What Would Jesus Do?

Making the Best Choices

OVER **150** CUSTOMIZING OPTIONS

SLASHER IV
THE FINAL REVENGE

SLASHER IV

SESSIONS THAT CHANGE • CUSTOM • CURRICULUM • TO FIT YOUR GROUP

5 Ready-to-Go **SESSIONS** with Reproducible Resources

Paul Borthwick
Stan Campbell

CUSTOM CURRICULUM

What Would Jesus Do?

Paul Borthwick

Stan Campbell

David C. Cook Church Ministries—Resources
A division of Cook Communications Ministries
Colorado Springs, CO/Paris, Ontario

Custom Curriculum
What Would Jesus Do?

Unless otherwise noted, Scripture quotations are from the Holy Bible, New International Version (NIV), © 1973, 1978, 1984 by International Bible Society. Used by permission of Zondervan Bible Publishers.

David C. Cook Church Ministries—Resources
A division of Cook Communications Ministries
4050 Lee Vance View; Colorado Springs, CO 80918-7100
Cable address: DCCOOK
Series creator: John Duckworth
Series editor: Randy Southern
Editor: Randy Southern
Option writers: Stan Campbell, Nelson E. Copeland, Jr., and Sue Reck
Designer: Bill Paetzold
Cover illustrator: Jere Smith
Inside illustrator: John Hayes
Printed in U.S.A.

ISBN: 0-7814-5156-6

C O N T E N T S

Sessions by Stan Campbell
Options by Stan Campbell, Nelson E. Copeland, Jr., and Sue Reck

About the Authors

Stan Campbell has been a youth worker for over nineteen years and has written several books on youth ministry including the BibleLog series (SonPower) and the Quick Studies series (David C. Cook). He and his wife, Pam, are youth directors at Lisle Bible Church in Lisle, Illinois.

Nelson E. Copeland, Jr., is a nationally known speaker and the author of several youth resources including *Great Games for City Kids* (Youth Specialties) and *A New Agenda for Urban Youth* (Winston-Derek). He is president of the Christian Education Coalition for African-American Leadership (CECAAL), an organization dedicated to reinforcing educational and cultural excellence among urban teenagers. He also serves as youth pastor at the First Baptist Church in Morton, Pennsylvania.

Sue Reck is an editor for Chariot Family Products. She is also a freelance curriculum writer. She has worked with young people in Sunday school classes, youth groups, and camp settings.

You've Made the Right Choice!

Thanks for choosing **Custom Curriculum!** We think your choice says at least three things about you:

(1) You know your group pretty well, and want your program to fit that group like a glove;

(2) You like having options instead of being boxed in by some far-off curriculum editor;

(3) You have a small mole on your left forearm, exactly two inches below the elbow.

OK, so we were wrong about the mole. But if you like having choices that help you tailor meetings to fit your kids, **Custom Curriculum** is the best place to be.

Going through Customs

In this (and every) **Custom Curriculum** volume, you'll find
• five great sessions you can use anytime, in any order.
• reproducible student handouts, at least one per session.
• a truckload of options for adapting the sessions to your group (more about that in a minute).
• a helpful get-you-ready article by a youth expert.
• clip art for making posters, fliers, and other kinds of publicity to get kids to your meetings.

Each **Custom Curriculum** session has three to six steps. No matter how many steps a session has, it's designed to achieve these goals:

• *Getting together.* Using an icebreaker activity, you'll help kids be glad they came to the meeting.

• *Getting thirsty.* Why should kids care about your topic? Why should they care what the Bible has to say about it? You'll want to take a few minutes to earn their interest before you start pouring the "living water."

• *Getting the Word.* By exploring and discussing carefully selected passages, you'll find out what God has to say.

• *Getting the point.* Here's where you'll help kids make the leap from principles to nitty-gritty situations they are likely to face.

• *Getting personal.* What should each group member do as a result of this session? You'll help each person find a specific "next step" response that works for him or her.

Each session is written to last 45 to 60 minutes. But what if you have less time—or more? No problem! **Custom Curriculum** is all about . . . options!

What Are My Options?

Every **Custom Curriculum** session gives you fourteen kinds of options:

- *Extra Action*—for groups that learn better when they're physically moving (instead of just reading, writing, and discussing).
- *Combined Junior High/High School*—to use when you're mixing age levels, and an activity or case study would be too "young" or "old" for part of the group.
- *Small Group*—for adapting activities that would be tough with groups of fewer than eight kids.
- *Large Group*—to alter steps for groups of more than twenty kids.
- *Urban*—for fitting sessions to urban facilities and multiethnic (especially African-American) concerns.
- *Heard It All Before*—for fresh approaches that get past the defenses of kids who are jaded by years in church.
- *Little Bible Background*—to use when most of your kids are strangers to the Bible, or haven't made a Christian commitment.
- *Mostly Guys*—to focus on guys' interests and to substitute activities they might be more enthused about.
- *Mostly Girls*—to address girls' concerns and to substitute activities they might prefer.
- *Extra Fun*—for longer, more "rowdy" youth meetings where the emphasis is on fun.
- *Short Meeting Time*—tips for condensing the session to 30 minutes or so.
- *Fellowship & Worship*—for building deeper relationships or enabling kids to praise God together.
- *Media*—to spice up meetings with video, music, or other popular media.
- *Sixth Grade*—appearing only in junior high/middle school volumes, this option helps you change steps that sixth graders might find hard to understand or relate to.
- *Extra Challenge*—appearing only in high school volumes, this option lets you crank up the voltage for kids who are ready for more Scripture or more demanding personal application.

Each kind of option is offered twice in each session. So in this book, you get *almost 150* ways to tweak the meetings to fit your group!

Customizing a Session

All right, you may be thinking. *With all of these options flying around, how do I put a session together? I don't have a lot of time, you know.*

We know! That's why we've made **Custom Curriculum** as easy to follow as possible. Let's take a look at how you might prepare an actual meeting. You can do that in four easy steps:

(1) *Read the basic session plan.* Start by choosing one or more of the goals listed at the beginning of the session. You have three to pick from: a goal that emphasizes *knowledge,* one that stresses *understanding,* and one that emphasizes *action.* Choose one or more, depending on what *you* want to accomplish. Then read the basic plan to see what will work for you and what might not.

(2) *Choose your options.* You don't *have* to use any options at all; the basic session plan would work well for many groups, and you may want

to stick with it if you have absolutely no time to consider options. But if you want a more perfect fit, check out your choices.

As you read the basic session plan, you'll see small symbols in the margin. Each symbol stands for a different kind of option. When you see a symbol, it means that kind of option is offered for that step. Turn to the options section (which can be found immediately following the Repro Resources for each session), look for the category indicated by the symbol, and you'll see that option explained.

Let's say you have a small group, mostly guys who get bored if they don't keep moving. You'll want to keep an eye out for three kinds of options: Small Group, Mostly Guys, and Extra Action. As you read the basic session, you might spot symbols that tell you there are Small Group options for Step 1 and Step 3—maybe a different way to play a game so that you don't need big teams, and a way to cover several Bible passages when just a few kids are looking them up. Then you see symbols telling you that there are Mostly Guys options for Step 2 and Step 4—perhaps a substitute activity that doesn't require too much self-disclosure, and a case study guys will relate to. Finally you see symbols indicating Extra Action options for Step 2 and Step 3—maybe an active way to get kids' opinions instead of handing out a survey, and a way to act out some verses instead of just looking them up.

After reading the options, you might decide to use four of them. You base your choices on your personal tastes and the traits of your group that you think are most important right now. **Custom Curriculum** offers you more options than you'll need, so you can pick your current favorites and plug others into future meetings if you like.

(3) *Use the checklist.* Once you've picked your options, keep track of them with the simple checklist that appears at the end of each option section (just before the start of the next session plan). This little form gives you a place to write down the materials you'll need too—since they depend on the options you've chosen.

(4) *Get your stuff together.* Gather your materials; photocopy any Repro Resources (reproducible student sheets) you've decided to use. And . . . you're ready!

The Custom Curriculum Challenge

Your kids are fortunate to have you as their leader. You see them not as a bunch of generic teenagers, but as real, live, unique kids. You care whether you really connect with them. That's why you're willing to take a few extra minutes to tailor your meetings to fit.

It's a challenge to work with real, live kids, isn't it? We think you deserve a standing ovation for taking that challenge. And we pray that **Custom Curriculum** helps you shape sessions that shape lives for Jesus Christ and His kingdom.

—The Editors

Living in a Multiple-Choice Society
by Paul Borthwick

Junior highers of the nineties make up what's been called the "multiple choice" generation. We are working with young people who are deluged with choices—from the mundane (dozens of cereal brands and potato chip varieties) to the extraordinarily profound (sexual preferences and moral convictions). Never before has a generation had so many alternatives from which to choose. Lifestyle options, elective classes, and 140 channel possibilities with just the touch of a remote all point to the myriad of selections facing today's junior higher.

Whether we're talking to young people about which videos to watch, whose value system to live by, or whose peer group to identify with, our goal is to help kids make the best possible decisions for their well-being—*from God's perspective.*

In the late nineteenth century, Charles Sheldon wrote a novel entitled *In His Steps.* Sheldon's goal was to translate the Christian life to people living in that era. In the book, he depicts the choices that citizens, business people, a newspaper editor, church leaders, and others would need to make in a non-Christian world. Throughout the book, he presents various challenges to the characters, forcing them to ask this basic question: "What would Jesus do in this situation?"

In the sessions that follow, your goal is similar to Sheldon's. Your challenge is to get your "characters"—your junior highers—to look at the real-life options they face and ask, "What would Jesus do?"

Foundations for Effectiveness

As you and your group study the tough questions in the sessions that follow, you should keep in mind two important suggestions.

First, *respect the intensity of your junior highers' feelings.* It's vitally important to remember that the issues you'll be studying are very profound in the lives of some of your junior highers. The starting point in leading these sessions is to take the issues and their impact on junior highers' lives seriously. Be empathetic.

One seventh grader came to ask me about cheating in school. Her questions made me wonder if she were just looking for me to justify her desire to get ahead by copying the work of others. I gave her a few glib answers and reminded her that cheating had no place in the life of a Christian. I thought I had settled the issue, but then she broke into tears.

"What's the matter?" I asked.

"Well, I don't know what to do," she said. "I believe that I shouldn't cheat, but my parents are putting so much pressure on me to get good grades that I'll either cheat and compromise my Christian faith or I won't cheat, and I'll get poor grades and disappoint my parents."

Her tears rebuked me. I realized that I had treated her lightly while she was dealing with a very tough decision.

The issues that follow carries varying levels of intensity in the lives of your kids. Some live daily with overly strict parents or an obnoxious older brother. Others feel that their social lives will suffer if they refuse to conform to the sexual standards of their peers. Some feel hostile toward the inconsistency at church. Others feel alone without friends.

Listen to your students as these issues are discussed. Young people will usually react most strongly to the issues that affect them most intensely. The sessions that follow will help you to discern which issues affect which kids most seriously.

On the opposite extreme, *look out for cluelessness!* In contrast to the young person who is intensely involved in a spiritual dilemma is the young person who never wrestles with questions of how the Christian faith applies to tough choices in daily life.

Three junior high guys told me on Sunday morning that they had refused to go to see an "R" rated movie with their peers on Friday night. I was proud of their choice so I asked them how they had come to this decision. I asked optimistically, "Did you explain to your friends that your commitment as a Christian prevented you from going to the movie?"

They looked at me blankly. "Heck no," replied one of the guys. "We told them that our parents would kill us if we went. The Christian thing never entered our minds."

These young men illustrate the way that a number of young people (and perhaps adults as well) live. To them, Christian faith relates to Sunday, to Bible study, and maybe to serving the needy—but it has no connection to the moral, ethical, and lifestyle choices of daily living.

The sessions that follow are designed to help kids in the "clueless" camp to connect their faith with their daily choices. Our tough task is to cause them to think, to remind them that following Jesus should affect their relationships at home, their pursuit of success or popularity at school, and their decision whether or not to drink alcohol.

As You Lead

The easiest way to address the tough choices facing kids is to *tell* kids what they should think and do. But our goal is more significant and long-term. We want to teach kids *how* to think, *how* to integrate their faith, and *how* to apply Christian discipleship to daily issues. If we can teach kids how to think, we'll give them skills that they can apply to other choices they'll be making throughout their lives.

The goal in all of the studies that follow is to teach decision-making skills from a biblical perspective. Rather than telling kids the opinions that we think they should have or the choices that we think they should make, our goal is to teach them how to examine Scripture (especially the life and teachings of Jesus) so that they make their own decisions based on personal, internalized convictions.

Here are some suggestions as to how you can go about this:

• *Think principles!* In the first century, Jesus did not need to decide about MTV, nor did He need to deal with cheating in school. As leaders, we need to be careful not to put words in Jesus' mouth. Instead of looking for definitive instructions on each issue, ask, "What principles apply to this decision?"

• *Develop your hooks.* Every teacher knows the value of a "hook." A hook might be a story, an illustration, a question, or a statement designed to get students' attention. Fashion some effective questions (perhaps with the help of a few junior high leadership students) that will stir some discussion on the topics. Try not to ask "leading" questions, the kind that discourage kids from offering an honest response. Instead of asking, "You don't think Jesus would go to an "R" rated movie, do you?" you might ask, "In light of what we know about Jesus, do you think He would go to an "R" rated movie? Why or why not?"

• *Be slow to speak.* Try not to reveal your personal feelings during a discussion, either by reacting negatively to far-out ideas or by speaking up too soon to relieve the silence. Allow kids to think, to wrestle, to debate the topics. During a youth group discussion on the Christian perspective on drinking alcohol, a young person raised a question about John 2, in which Jesus made wine at the wedding banquet. The youth leader jumped on the student and rebuked his insights as being naive and biblically unfounded. The youth leader's hasty response turned off the group members. Rather than wrestling with the issue, the kids began to think that the youth leader was embarrassed by Jesus' action and was "covering" for Him. Perhaps it would have been better to allow the discussion to proceed and encourage group members to decide for themselves—based on the entire life of Jesus.

The Bottom Line

In tackling the tough questions that follow, our goal is to produce group members who understand that the Christian life involves discernment, moderation, and wisdom.

Discernment involves kids understanding for themselves how to choose between good and evil. Hebrews 5:14 informs us that discernment comes to those who "by constant use have trained themselves to distinguish good from evil." Therefore, youth ministry should include "training" sessions in which kids can wrestle with "What would Jesus do?" questions so that they're able to discern the best choices to make.

Moderation involves understanding that even though some things may not be directly destructive, they still might not be the best course of action. We want to develop Christian young people who can say with Paul, "'Everything is permissible for me'—but not everything is beneficial. 'Everything is permissible for me'—but I will not be mastered by anything" (1 Corinthians 6:12).

In our complicated world, one of the best things we can do for young people is to teach them to ask God for wisdom according to James 1:5. We serve the best interests of students by teaching them to look to God for insight to make the best possible choices in the midst of hundreds of options. May God richly bless you as you help your kids answer the question "What would Jesus do?"

Paul Borthwick is minister of missions at Grace Chapel in Lexington, Massachusetts. A former youth pastor and frequent speaker to youth workers, he is author of several books including Organizing Your Youth Ministry *and* Feeding Your Forgotten Soul: Spiritual Growth for Youth Workers *(Zondervan).*

The images on these two pages are designed to help you promote this course within your church and community. Feel free to photocopy anything here and adapt it to fit your publicity needs. The stuff on this page could be used as a flier that you send or hand out to kids—or as a bulletin insert. The stuff on the next page could be used to add visual interest to newsletters, calendars, bulletin boards, or other promotions. Be creative and have fun!

What If . . .

What if Jesus went to your school? What if He hung around with your friends? What if He had to live with your family? What if He attended your church? These are some of the questions we'll be exploring in a new course called *What Would Jesus Do?* By looking at Christ's example, you can get some valuable tips for living your own life!

Who:

When:

Where:

Questions? Call:

What Would Jesus Do?

What Would Jesus Do?

Bored? Looking for something exciting in your life?

Bring a friend.

It's party time!

What Would Jesus Do
. . . for Fun?

YOUR GOALS FOR THIS SESSION:

Choose one or more

☐ To help kids see that if they aren't careful, many of their fun activities can become temptations.

☐ To help kids understand that genuine fun is generated from a positive attitude and should not depend on other personalities or external circumstances.

☐ To help kids evaluate the amount of fun they have in various areas of their lives and attempt to have more genuine fun wherever they are.

☐ Other _____

Your Bible Base:

Matthew 4:1-11
Luke 7:36-50
Colossians 3:17

A Really Good Day

(Needed: Paper, pencils)

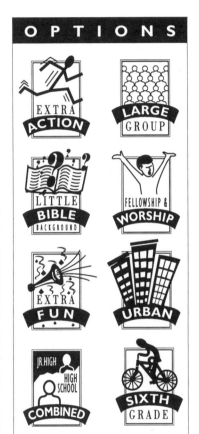
Hand out paper and pencils as kids arrive. Ask them to write down what they would consider to be an almost perfect day. Their descriptions should be as detailed as possible. For example, ask: **What would be your schedule, from morning to night? Where would you go? Who would you be with? What season would it be? What temperature would it be? What music would you be listening to?**

Explain that you're not looking for descriptions of wild and imaginative fantasy days in which kids have breakfast on the surf in Hawaii and then fly to Rio for lunch. Rather, you're looking for descriptions of things that group members have actually experienced or would at least have a shot at doing someday.

When kids are finished, collect their written descriptions. Read a few at random and let group members guess who wrote each one. In most cases, kids are likely to describe positive and innocent activities. In this context, few people are likely to include things such as drinking, sexual activity, or similar behaviors. Yet many young people—including Christian young people—get involved in such things, supposedly with the goal of having "fun." Point out that we can plan "perfect" days that don't include drinking, drugs, sex, or other potential pitfalls. Keep this in mind as you continue the session.

A Partying of the Ways

(Needed: Copies of Repro Resource 1)

Hand out copies of "Party Time!" (Repro Resource 1). Assign the roles to various group members. (All group members without individual parts can join the "Party Animals" chant.) Read the skit as a group.

Afterward, ask: **Would you go to this party? Why or why not?**
Have you ever had an opportunity to go to a party similar to this one? Did you go? If so, what was it like? Did you enjoy yourself?
How do you feel when you're with a group of people who suddenly begin to have "fun" by doing things you aren't really comfortable doing?
Do you think Jesus would go to the party described in the skit? Why or why not?
What do you think Jesus did for fun?

Encourage several group members to respond to each of these questions. Many of your young people might be surprised to learn that Jesus attended parties where alcohol and prostitutes were present. In fact, His first recorded miracle is providing wine for a wedding where the supply had run out (John 2:1-11). It may be hard for some people to picture Jesus in such a setting, since they know He lived a sinless life. They need to see the importance of learning how He could be exposed to booze and hookers, yet never get drunk nor commit a sexual sin.

Well-meaning Bible teachers may have painted an incomplete picture of Jesus for students. In emphasizing how He never approved of sin, some teachers may have given the impression that He disapproved of sinners as well. So make sure your group members are aware that crowds flocked around Jesus wherever He went. He hugged small children, even when His disciples tried to shoo them away. He touched lepers. He tried to open people's minds and free them from the restricted thinking of their religious leaders. All in all, Jesus certainly must have been a fun person to be around. Sure, He came to earth on a serious and solemn mission, but His mission didn't cause His personal relationships with people to be dull or gloomy.

STEP
3

Invitations and Temptations

(Needed: Bibles)

Explain: **Since Jesus was able to spend time at parties and around sinful people, yet remain sinless Himself, He must have had a different perspective than many of us have. Let's try to see what His "secret" might have been.**

Have kids form two groups. Instruct Group #1 to read and discuss

Matthew 4:1-11, which describes Jesus' temptations in the desert. Instruct Group #2 to read and discuss Luke 7:36-50, the account of Jesus at a Pharisee's dinner party. Each group should prepare to report on its assignment, either verbally or by acting out the story. Explain that after the groups report, you'll try to find a balance for having fun without crossing the line into sinful activity.

The members of Group #1 should discover that Jesus' life certainly involved a lot more than going to parties. One of the first things He did as He prepared to begin His public ministry was go into the desert and face severe temptations. He fasted forty days and nights, and was (not surprisingly) very hungry. Satan's first temptation was something to the effect of "I dare you to turn these stones into bread." And while there was nothing wrong with Jesus getting something to eat, He never used His power to make Himself more comfortable. Satan's second temptation was for Jesus to plunge from the top of a tall building, which would have manipulated God into saving Him. Jesus declined again, refusing to call attention to Himself simply because He might be able to do so. And finally, Satan tried to play "Let's Make a Deal" by offering Jesus kingdoms and possessions. But Jesus knew what was really important in life and told Satan to get lost. His experience of hunger and temptation was certainly not a pleasant experience, yet it brought Him closer to God, His father. Going to a few parties during this forty-day period might have been a lot more fun, but Jesus realized that this was the time to do something necessary and beneficial—for Himself and others.

The members of Group #2 will see another side of Jesus' life as they describe His behavior at a dinner party thrown by a Pharisee named Simon. It was supposed to be a quiet dinner with the Pharisee, a few of his friends, and Jesus. But it was crashed by a prostitute who came up behind Jesus and started to cry. She used her tears to wash His feet and her hair to dry them. Then she kissed His feet and anointed them with perfume. As this was going on, Simon was becoming more skeptical about Jesus, assuming that He didn't know this was a "woman of ill repute." But Jesus knew all about the woman, and He knew Simon's thoughts as well. He told a parable to try to teach the guests a lesson, He forgave the woman's sins and astounded the people at the party.

After both groups have reported, say: **Jesus' temptations were all very much like "dares" from Satan—to use His power selfishly, to call attention to Himself, and to sacrifice His relationship with God in order to pick up a few material possessions. What are some dares people your age may receive today?** If no one mentions it, point out that introductions to drinking, sex, drugs, and other harmful behaviors often come through dares. Explain that sometimes it requires more strength and courage to decline the dare than to go through with it. The temptation Jesus faced from Satan is sort of a form of peer pressure—much as we might face from our own peers.

Jesus' temptations came at a vulnerable time—after He had left home to begin His ministry and before He had assembled His disciples. What potential temptations might you face as you become more independent of your parents? (Opportunities for drinking and sex usually become available. Also, priorities to get ahead "at any cost" and other detrimental attitudes may develop during this time if people don't continue to seek and obey God's will.)

In which of the previous stories do you think Jesus had more fun: fasting in the wilderness or attending the Pharisee's party? Let a few kids offer their opinions. You might want to suggest that He was equally content since He was following God's will in both cases. We may have come to perceive church as boring and parties as fun, but neither case is necessarily true. The rest of the session will try to show that fun is determined more by the attitude we choose than by a particular set of circumstances.

Which do you think was more important for Jesus: spending time alone with God or spending time with people? (Both are important. Either one without the other leads to a life that gets out of balance.)

Why do you think Jesus was able to act so kindly toward the prostitute at the party? (Perhaps because He had first spent a lot of time with God and had learned to deal with temptation. He didn't go to parties to "let His hair down." Rather, He was consistent in His character and His faith, whether alone with God His Father or in a crowd of people.)

Do you think it's possible for *us* to be as balanced as Jesus—to go to parties and have a genuine love and concern for other people, yet not get caught up in the sins that others might be participating in? (Certainly it is possible, but only if we are as committed to obeying God as Jesus was.) It needs to be pointed out that Jesus was a legal adult. For your junior highers, drinking and related activities are not only bad [sinful] habits, they are illegal as well.

Pushing Fun to the Limits

Explain that some pursuits of "fun" are obviously wrong. When young people turn to alcohol, drugs, sexual activity, and such, the immediate sensations may indeed seem thrilling. But the satisfaction provided by such things quickly begins to diminish. Only too late do most people discover the "fun" is in the blatant defiance of what is expected of them, not so much in the activities themselves. A hangover, a sexually transmitted disease, an unwanted baby, or an addiction will quickly bring fun to an end. It is much better to seek other alternatives for fun and entertainment. Yet *anything* that is repeated too frequently can lose its allure. A hot fudge sundae can be a fun treat. But if all a person eats is hot fudge sundaes, they soon cease to be so satisfying.

The following is a list of things young people do for fun. Read the activities one at a time and let group members rate each one from one (least) to ten (most) in regard to how much fun it is. Have kids respond by holding up an appropriate number of fingers to show their ratings.

- **Bungee jumping**
- **Video or computer games**
- **MTV**
- **G-rated movies**
- **PG-rated movies**
- **R-rated movies**
- **Softball**
- **Volleyball**
- **Football**
- **Miniature golf**
- **Bowling**
- **Youth group**
- **Church**
- **School**
- **Homework**
- **Going to the mall**
- **Bible study**
- **Prayer**
- **Waterskiing**
- **Swimming**
- **Going to an amusement park**
- **Listening to music**

• Going on a date

Add activities to the list that you know some of your kids like to do. Also let group members offer suggestions of things they really enjoy that weren't included on the list.

Then ask: **Of all these fun things, do you think any of them could ever become a temptation that might cause you to sin? If so, in what ways?** Discussion might begin with things that are associated with these activities. For example, movies can expose kids to illicit sex, violence, profanity, and other nonbiblical behaviors. But at a different level, many of these things can become addictive in the sense of taking time that could be better spent doing something more constructive. We tend to recognize this problem more in things such as video or computer games, watching TV, and so forth. Yet some people go to the lake to water-ski every weekend during the summer—even on Sunday mornings when they could be in church. Many sports, especially organized sports in school, can prevent kids from attending youth group, retreats, or other beneficial activities. It's always easier to choose to do something "fun" than something we know we *should* do, such as a church function. (Again, this is where one's personal attitude comes into the picture.)

How can we participate in all of these good, fun activities, yet keep from letting them become temptations for us? (We need to follow Jesus' example. Fun activities remain fun as long as we don't neglect our relationship with God. When we make spiritual development our highest priority, fun usually takes care of itself.) Point out that even though Jesus was usually swarmed by people who wanted His healing, His company, or some other favor, He still made time to be alone with God. Sometimes it had to be "very early in the morning, while it was still dark" (Mark 1:35), but it remained a priority for Him. Consequently, He could go to parties and talk with people without losing sight of who He was or what was most important in His life. He could associate with sinners, yet keep Himself detached from sin. We need to learn to do the same.

Make Your Own Fun Wherever You Go

(Needed: Bibles, copies of Repro Resource 2, pencils)

O P T I O N S

So far the emphasis has been on *what* is fun and what isn't. Before the session ends, you need to cover some of the *whos* and *wheres*.

Ask: **Do you know people who, whenever you are with them, always seem to find something fun for the two of you to do?**

Do you have some favorite places that, whenever you go there, you almost always have a lot of fun?

In contrast, are there people or places that seem to drain the fun right out of you?

Hand out copies of "A Measure of Fun" (Repro Resource 2) and pencils. Kids will be asked to evaluate how much fun they have at various places (math class, church, etc.). They will also be asked to set some goals for how they can make their least fun places more of a joy than usual. After most of your group members have completed the sheet, discuss their responses and goals.

Then summarize: **Many times the main reason we don't have fun someplace is because we choose not to have fun. We tell ourselves, *Oh, crud, I have to go to church—or school, or wherever—this morning. What a waste. I could be doing so many other fun things instead.* But what if we changed our attitude a bit and, before going, told ourselves, *All right! I get to go to church—or school, or wherever—this morning. I'm going to be the most fun person there. In fact, I'm going to be so much fun that it's going to rub off on everyone else.* If you had that attitude, how might it make a big difference?**

Close with a challenge for group members not to take your word for it, but to try this approach this week and see for themselves. To help them remember how important a good attitude is, have someone read Colossians 3:17: "And whatever you do, whether in word or deed, do it all in the name of the Lord Jesus, giving thanks to God the Father through him." If time permits, have your group members memorize this verse before leaving. Explain that thankful people are fun people. As we learn to appreciate the good things around us (wherever we are), we learn to maintain a higher level of joy (fun) no matter what else happens.

PARTY TIME!

PARTY ANIMALS (*running around the room, chanting*): Par-*tee*! Par-*tee*! Par-*tee*!

PAT: Hey, Chris! Are you going to Joe's party tomorrow night?

CHRIS: Are you kidding?! From what I hear, the whole school is going to be there—at least everyone who was invited.

PAT: And several who weren't.

PARTY ANIMALS (*still running around*): Par-*tee*! Par-*tee*! Par-*tee*!

(*STEVE and GINNY enter.*)

STEVE: Hi, guys! Are you guys going to Joe's party?

PAT AND CHRIS: For sure!

GINNY: This should be great! I hear his parents are out of town—for three weeks!

STEVE: And I hear they have an *excellent* liquor cabinet.

GINNY: Who needs it? Practically everyone is bringing a six-pack—or a bottle of *something*.

CHRIS: And I hear Joe is inviting a lot of girls who are . . . let's just say, *very friendly*—if you know what I mean. They're all going to be there!

GINNY: And Joe's guy friends aren't too shabby either! Some of them are really rich.

PARTY ANIMALS (*still running around*): Par-*tee*! Par-*tee*! Par-*tee*!

PAT: There go some of them now—fine specimens of humanity, they are.

CHRIS: Wow! A party with all of our friends.

GINNY: All of the cool people from school, tons of food—

PAT: Free-flowing beer and who knows what else—

STEVE: And plenty of "easy" girls! Who could possibly pass this one up?

CHRIS: You said it. There's only one word for this big event.

EVERYONE: Par-*tee*! Par-*tee*! Par-*tee*!

A Measure of Fun

Gas gauges on cars come in pretty handy. They let you know at any point how much fuel you have on hand, so you can stock up again before you run completely out. Wouldn't it be good to have gauges to help us measure fun? If we aren't careful, we can be at a place that *should* be a lot of fun, yet suddenly discover that we're running dangerously low—or may be completely out. So think of each of the following places and "take a reading" of your fun level in each one. Draw the needle in the appropriate place to show how full of fun you are (or how close you are to empty). Then, for any of these areas in which you aren't at least three-quarters full, think of some ways that *you* can take the initiative and create more fun on a regular basis.

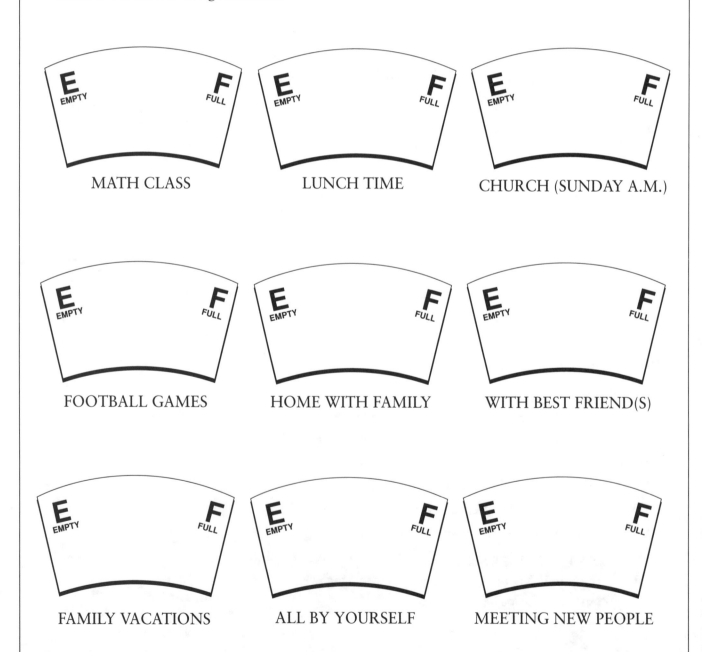

MATH CLASS

LUNCH TIME

CHURCH (SUNDAY A.M.)

FOOTBALL GAMES

HOME WITH FAMILY

WITH BEST FRIEND(S)

FAMILY VACATIONS

ALL BY YOURSELF

MEETING NEW PEOPLE

EXTRA ACTION

Step 1

To begin the session, have each group member think of one of his or her favorite activities. However, the person should not mention what that activity is. Ask your group members to form a large circle, facing inward. Then, at your signal, have them simultaneously begin to pantomime the activities they have in mind. (Each person should act out only one activity.) Continue this for about a minute, while each person looks around the circle and tries to identify what everyone else is doing. After your signal to stop, let group members try to guess what each person was pantomiming. Then begin the session as written.

Step 4

As you're discussing how "innocent" activities can turn into temptations, have kids form groups. Instruct each group to create a skit to demonstrate how innocent activities can become dangerous. Point out that while group members' initial tendency may be to use the activities listed in the session and think in terms of their own age-group, they need not do so. For example, a skit might involve a four-year-old girl asking Dad (who is not paying much attention to her) for permission to play with his chain saw. Group members should see that while there is nothing wrong with a chain saw, there are certain commonsense principles that should govern its use. The same should be true of watching television, playing videos, involvement in sports, or anything else you've discussed.

SMALL GROUP

Step 3

One advantage of a small group is that you can cover more material together and still hold everyone's attention. So rather than dividing your already small group in half to cover the two Bible stories, do them both as a single group. Both of these stories can be read as narratives by assigning various group members the quoted statements (Jesus, Satan, Simon, etc.) and designating someone else as narrator to read all of the non-quoted passages. This method will help bring the Bible characters to life—and will also help readers pay attention (so they'll be ready with their parts).

Step 5

At the end of this session on fun, plan to do something new and different—either at your next meeting or sometime during the week. A small group should have less trouble planning something on short notice because there are fewer schedules to consider. One popular activity is a progressive dinner. Pack everyone into a car or van and make a stop at each person's house before the evening is over. Plan to have appetizers at the first house, salad at the second house, soup at the third house, followed by the main course, dessert, after-dinner hot cider, and so forth. Small groups need different and exciting outings as much as larger ones, but sometimes the small numbers don't seem "worth the effort." If a spirit of excitement can be generated among the few who are there, usually others will eventually be invited to attend, and the group will begin to grow.

LARGE GROUP

Step 1

Rather than having kids write descriptions of an ideal day and then guessing who wrote what, set up a "Temptation Table." Prior to the session, display several of your kids' favorite foods on a table where everyone is certain to see them. The foods should include things like cookies or candies (things that can be "sampled" without being noticed) rather than cakes or pies. Put a sign on the table that reads "Do Not Touch." As kids arrive, adult leaders should be nowhere in sight. Also prear-range for one group member to be a tempter. He or she should stand near the table and make comments about how delicious the food looks. If no one succumbs to initial temptations, the tempter might nibble on some of the treats and see if anyone follows suit. When the adult leaders finally show up, they should have a number of even better treats as rewards for anyone who withstood the Temptation Table. Afterward, point out that while sweets can be fun treats under the right circumstances, they can also serve as temptations for us. Like other fun things, we need to prevent them from becoming temptations for us.

Step 5

It can be overwhelming to try to ensure that a large group is having fun on a regular basis—so let kids share the responsibility. At the end of the session, have kids form groups. Designate each group as a "fun team." Explain that the fun teams will plan fun events for future sessions on a rotating basis. These should be simple one- or two-minute events (games, jokes, riddles, skits, etc.). The only requirements are that they be clean and fun. Encourage the fun teams to be creative. Some might demonstrate "Stupid Human Tricks" (strange talents), put together a jug band, or whatever. The weirder (and "funner"), the better. Let the fun teams begin to brainstorm ideas during this session. Then assign the first "rotation" of dates when each team should be expected to provide the fun.

HEARD IT ALL
BEFORE

FELLOWSHIP &
WORSHIP

Step 2

As part of your discussion after reading the skit on Repro Resource 1, ask: **What would you say was the most surprising thing Jesus ever did?** Let each person respond. If your group members know the Bible well, they should provide a number of answers (walk on water, turn water to wine, rise from the dead, bring a major storm to a dead stop, etc.). Ask: **How do you think these surprising things affected the thinking of people around Jesus?** Point out that Jesus frequently "broke the mold" of traditional thinking. Among other things, this tendency probably created an atmosphere of fun. While everything probably was not "ha ha" humorous, there is something thrilling about not knowing what might happen next. Explain that when we tend to get in a rut, we may need to draw closer to God and see what unexpected things He might have in store for us.

Step 3

After the Bible study groups have read and discussed their assigned stories, begin a debate. One group should defend the position that Jesus was most committed to personal spiritual integrity. The other group should argue that Jesus placed more emphasis on people and relationships (fun). Groups may draw on the Scripture passages they read as well as any others that might help make their points. Since many junior highers won't be familiar with traditional debate procedure, you might want to provide opportunities for rebuttal and/or ask questions for clarification. It should become clear through the debate (with a little additional comment from you) that Jesus placed great importance on both personal spiritual commitment *and* other people and their needs. We should do the same. People and fun are important, but not at the expense of our own individual growth.

Step 1

Before moving on to Step 2, pass around something sticky or wet (a popcorn ball, a wet paper towel, a fish from the grocery store, etc.). Make sure everyone handles the object at least once. Then ask: **Even though you "passed on" this object when you came into contact with it, were you affected in any way?** Kids should see that even though they may have tried to remain "unaffected," they still retained a residual effect from the object (a smell that rubbed off, a bit of moisture, or whatever). Point out that they need to be careful about even *approaching* certain activities—whether or not they actually get involved—because they may be more influenced by such things than they think. Kids may be learning that certain activities are right and others are wrong, but they still need help developing a sense of spiritual discernment to determine when they may be in more danger than they can see.

Step 3

Because so many young people have an incomplete picture of who Jesus is, spend some time helping your kids fill in the gaps. One way to do this is to have them think of three to five people they most admire. Then have them determine exactly what it is about each of those people that captures their respect. It could be that Dad provides unconditional love. A teacher might go out of her way to help the student learn. An uncle might be a role model in a specific job the kid has an interest in. After listing all of the qualities of their human role models, have group members consider whether or not Jesus fits those same criteria. In most cases, you should be able to think of an instance from Jesus' life that reflects any good or admirable quality. Help your group members see that whatever they are looking to emulate, Jesus stands as the best possible example.

Step 1

To help increase the level of fellowship in your group, ask one of your group members a few days before the session to read and prepare a brief report on some good resource materials that promote fun in relation to Christianity. The best way to locate such resources is to wander around a local Christian bookstore until you find something that looks promising. One example is Tony Campolo's book, *The Kingdom of God Is a Party* (Word). You might assign someone to read and report on Chapter 6: "Turning Church into a Party." Your volunteer can pass along interesting anecdotes as well as challenges laid out by the author. Many resources also provide good, fun activities to try as well. Look until you find something that's right for your group. Then choose the right person to present the material, someone who can make something happen to liven up your group.

Step 5

At the end of the session, have your group members brainstorm things they can do to help make their *worship* more fun. There are times to be serious and meditative, certainly, but there are also times to "cut loose" in their praise and worship of God. If this can be done at a congregational level, challenge them to do so. Some of their livelier songs and a few skits or short plays can bring a lot of life to a church service. But if your kids don't have such an opportunity, have them plan a fun worship service among themselves. Make sure all of the elements of worship are included: music, Bible study, fellowship, and so forth. However, each of these things should be conducted in an innovative and enjoyable way. Remember to keep your focus on God. We worship not to have fun, but to glorify Him. But fun can be a by-product of worship.

MOSTLY GIRLS

Step 2

In a group of mostly girls, you may need to make some adjustments to the skit on Repro Resource 1. To start with, you may want to change the character named "Steve" to "Jill." You may also want to change "Joe's party" to "Kristy's party." Instead of having your actors talk about the "very friendly" or "easy" girls who will be at the party, have them discuss the "studly guys" who will be there.

Step 4

Have your girls brainstorm a list of the "fun-tations" (fun activities that could turn into temptations) that could become a problem for them. Write group members' suggestions on the board as they are named. After you've got several ideas listed, have your girls narrow the choices to create a "top ten list." Then, as a group, talk about specific things your girls can do to help keep fun activities fun, without letting them become temptations.

MOSTLY GUYS

Step 3

After you discuss Jesus' temptations, have each of your guys describe "The Dumbest Dare I Ever Took." At some point in their lives, most junior high guys have taken some pretty stupid dares (eating certain foods, taking physical risks, etc.). Try to get some stories started. Once a couple of guys speak up, others should begin to recall similar incidents. Focus on the *consequences* of their actions. Point out through their stories that while we sometimes "get by with" certain actions that aren't so smart, we should become more careful as we get older. The dares (temptations) become more dangerous. A dare to split a six-pack with a friend might be accepted if the perceived consequences only include getting caught by parents or perhaps the police. But few young people ever suspect that other risks include a lifetime of addiction or the possibility of harming someone while in a drunken state. Also discuss how anyone who continues to be motivated by dares is always at the mercy of others. By the time a kid is in junior high, he needs to realize that it takes more strength and sense to turn down certain dares than to feel compelled to "prove his manhood" by taking needless risks.

Step 4

After addressing needless risks in Step 3, plan an *acceptable* risky endeavor in this step. As you discuss things your guys consider fun, listen for things they might like to try. Then actually plan to do one or more of those things as a group. Most guys would look forward to the adventure of canoeing, rafting, mountain climbing, fishing, camping, or similar activities. It's easy to *ask* them not to get involved in certain activities. It's more work (but also more effective) to provide adventurous activities that are OK for them to do. Yet if your guys are given sufficient challenges in "safe" settings, they will probably be far less likely to try to manufacture excitement on their own by means of potentially dangerous and undesirable activities.

EXTRA FUN

Step 1

Begin the session with a "celebrity" version of the opening activity. Have each person choose a celebrity (real or fictional) and write down at least three activities that would make up an "almost perfect" day for that person. The rest of the group members will then try to guess the celebrity based on the list of activities. For instance, someone might come up with these three activities: "(1) Take Betty out for some Bronto Burgers. (2) Work on the car while my son holds it up. (3) Beat Fred in three straight games of bowling." The rest of the group members would probably guess that the celebrity being described is Barney Rubble (of *The Flintstones*).

Step 4

Your kids are probably familiar with the Beach Boys' song, "Fun, Fun, Fun." As you discuss how certain things can start out as fun but then lose their allure or become addictive, ask: **What are some things that tend to ruin fun activities for you?** Don't have kids answer aloud, but have everyone think of an answer. Then mention the Beach Boys song and remind everyone that the original complaint was "We'll have fun, fun, fun till her daddy takes the T-Bird away." That's what brought *their* fun to an end. Sing the lines a couple of times so everyone can see how the tune goes. Then explain that, as a group, you're going to keep singing, "We'll have fun, fun, fun till . . ." and then you'll point to someone to finish the line (singing or speaking) with his or her specific answer. Keep singing and pointing to people until everyone has had a chance to respond. Then ask: **Do you want to have fun all of the time? Do you think we should have fun all of the time? Is it necessarily a bad thing when fun comes to an end?** Kids should see that anything that happens all of the time ceases to be fun. Truly fun events may be those things that occur at repeated, but limited, intervals. They are things that can be looked forward to and then recalled with fondness.

Step 3

Provide group members with a variety of magazines and newspapers. Instruct group members to find a number of ads that portray potentially harmful activities (such as drinking or smoking) as fun activities. Then ask everyone to look for "opposites" to these proposed fun benefits. For example, a photo of a gorgeous model seductively holding a cigarette can be countered with an article or obituary notice referring to lung cancer, the effects of secondary smoke, etc. An enticing ad for alcohol might be contrasted with a photo of a drunk person lying in an alley. Media are used effectively to promote certain products that can have disastrous effects. If possible, use those same media to show the other side of such "fun" products or activities.

Step 4

A frequently overlooked form of media is T-shirts; yet most people wear T-shirts that promote the products and/or activities they think are fun (concerts, beer, sex, sports, etc.). If possible, take your group members to a mall or other public place to let them see how many different T-shirt "billboards" they can find. Have them list all of the products, activities, or places they find mentioned on other people's T-shirts. If a field trip is out of the question, have kids think of T-shirts they own or have seen recently that captured their attention. Most kids should be able to name several from memory. Then ask: **When people look at you, do you suppose they ever think that you must find church and/or youth group to be a fun place? Do you think they can see any excitement about being a Christian simply from watching your life? Why or why not?** As group members notice the T-shirts other people wear with pride that promote footwear, vacation spots, or whatever, challenge them to promote their faith—not just with catchy slogans on their clothing, but with their very lives.

Step 2

Combine Steps 1 and 2 with the following activity. Write several dates on the board. These dates should span history and include the future—5000 B.C., 4 B.C., A.D. 800, 1492, 1984, 2000, 2431, etc. Have kids form groups. Assign each group one of the dates on the board. Instruct the members of each group to explain (or act out) what kids their age probably did (or will do) for fun in their assigned year. For instance, kids in 5000 B.C. might have wrestled baby dinosaurs. Kids in A.D. 2431 might cruise around in their own spaceship. After a few minutes, have each group share what it came up with. Afterward, ask: **What do you think Jesus did for fun?** Encourage several responses. Then move on to Step 3.

Step 5

Rather than having kids take time to fill out Repro Resource 2, you can cover the material in a speedier way. Ask for two volunteers from the group. Explain that you're going to name a place or situation. When you do, your two volunteers must start suggesting ways to make that place or situation more fun. The first volunteer will have five seconds to make a suggestion; then the second volunteer will have five seconds to make another suggestion. The two will continue until one of them can't think of a new suggestion (within the time limit). Declare the other person the winner and award him or her a prize. Then ask for two more volunteers to play the next round. Play as many rounds as you have time for, using the places and situations on Repro Resource 2.

Step 1

After your group members describe their "almost perfect day," have them describe a typical *night* in their life. How do your city kids spend the hours between 8:00 p.m. and 6:00 a.m.? Do they hang out with friends, getting into trouble? Or do they use that time for homework and rest? Make the point that what a person does during the nighttime hours greatly affects what he or she can accomplish during the daytime. In other words, an "almost perfect day" requires a well-spent night. Get a feel for how much sleep (on average) your group members get every night. For fun, you might want to use the following "grading scale":

• 1-2 hours—You're a dead head.
• 3-4 hours—You're a yawning fool.
• 5-6 hours—You're an afternoon dozer.
• 7-8 hours—You're a quality sleeper.
• 9-10 hours—You're sleeping your life away!

   [NOTE: This grading scale is based on the assumption that 7-8 hours of sleep per night is ideal. Of course, some people require less sleep than that; others require more. You may want to adjust the scale to better reflect your group members' sleeping habits.]

Step 5

After discussing the scenarios on Repro Resource 2, ask your group to brainstorm some ways to have fun in the following situations:

• **Because of heavy gang violence in your neighborhood, you have to stay inside your house or apartment after school and during the weekend.**
• **Your local basketball court and community center are being torn down to make way for a new office building.**
• **You find out you have to take summer school.**

COMBINED (JR. HIGH / HIGH SCHOOL)

Step 1
To begin the session, ask: **What things did you think were really fun a year or two ago that you don't particularly enjoy today?** Let your junior highers respond first, and then your high schoolers. What your group members might discover is that an activity can mean a lot to them for a while, but over time, the excitement of that activity can fade—or even disappear. Some of the responses of your high schoolers may surprise your junior highers. The younger kids may just be discovering the joy of certain things that the older ones have already "burned out" on. If so, make the point that throughout life, certain things are going to be fun for a time. But if they're not enjoyed in moderation, they may become nothing more than occasional pastimes or mere memories.

Step 2
It may be difficult for your junior highers to agree with high schoolers (who may be more mature and sophisticated) on activities they both consider to be fun. But after going through the skit and discussing the questions in Step 2, have your group members create a list of "elements of a great party." Agree ahead of time that nothing goes on the list unless a majority of both junior highers and high schoolers agree to it. Then after you compile the list, plan the party! Divide the responsibilities so that all of the elements will be included. Someone can volunteer to get the "right" music. Others can sign up to arrange favorite kinds of foods. If a special location is needed (such as a gymnasium or swimming pool), have someone agree to make some calls and line up a place. It's one thing to teach about what constitutes fun. The important thing is that you model it and show that some things can be equally enjoyed by any age-group.

SIXTH GRADE

Step 1
Rather than having group members write out what a perfect day would be like for them, provide some paper and an assortment of markers, crayons, paints, and other art supplies. Ask group members to *draw* a perfect day and then be prepared to describe it to the rest of the group. Give the kids a few minutes to work. When everyone is finished, have group members explain what they've drawn and describe the emotions, activities, and so forth that they couldn't express artistically.

Step 5
As you wrap up the session, ask: **How do you think your definition of fun will change by the time you're in high school? What things will you think are fun then that you aren't able to do today?** One of the major goals of many young kids is driving, although sixth graders still have several years to wait and may not even be thinking seriously about it at this time. Sometimes you'll get some interesting answers by asking young people to speculate about the future. Their answers are likely to alert you to what the older people in their lives consider to be fun activities. Assure group members that they'll be able to do more "adult" things soon enough. Then encourage them to look for new and exciting things they can do as sixth graders. Later in life they may be surprised to remember exactly how much fun those things were (even if such things don't seem so special right now).

PLANNING CHECKLIST

Date Used:

Approx.
Time

Step 1: A Really Good Day _____
o Extra Action
o Large Group
o Little Bible Background
o Fellowship & Worship
o Extra Fun
o Urban
o Combined Jr. High/High School
o Sixth Grade

Step 2: A Partying of the Ways _____
o Heard It All Before
o Mostly Girls
o Short Meeting Time
o Combined Jr. High/High School

Step 3: Invitations and Temptations _____
o Small Group
o Heard It All Before
o Little Bible Background
o Mostly Guys
o Media

Step 4: Pushing Fun to the Limits _____
o Extra Action
o Mostly Girls
o Mostly Guys
o Extra Fun
o Media

Step 5: Make Your Own Fun Wherever You Go _____
o Small Group
o Large Group
o Fellowship & Worship
o Short Meeting Time
o Urban
o Sixth Grade

2 What Would Jesus Do . . . at My School?

Choose one or more

☐ To help kids imagine what Jesus might have been like as a junior high student in a school similar to theirs.

☐ To help kids understand that they should begin now to demonstrate their faith—at school as well as at church.

☐ To help kids see that a get-ahead-at-any-cost mentality will prevent spiritual growth, and to challenge them to set goals to become more servant-minded.

☐ Other _____
_____

Your Bible Base:

Matthew 20:20-28
Luke 2:41-52

Whatever It Takes

To begin the session, have group members form teams. Instruct each team to plan a skit. In the skit, one person should have a goal that he or she is desperate to accomplish. Other group members may portray teachers, parents, other adults, fellow students, etc. The skits should show the extreme lengths that kids go to in order to do something they feel driven to do. Explain that the skits need not reflect what your specific group members would necessarily do (since they are so good and pure), but rather what lengths *other* desperate junior highers might go to. Some of the skits might include the following scenarios:

• Someone is desperate to make an A in a class that he or she has never made better than a C in. (Options might include recruiting study partners, finding a tutor, copying homework, cheating on tests, changing the teacher's grade book, attempted bribery, etc.)

• Someone wants to break into a snooty clique at school. (He or she might pester members, buy gifts for key people, ditch existing friends, act in a manner completely opposite to his or her true personality, etc.)

• A football player who sits on the bench all of the time wants to get into a game. (He could follow the coach around, try to trip and injure one of the other players, do exercises continually on the sideline to get noticed, trade jerseys with another player to get on the field, etc.)

• Someone wants to get rid of a nerdy friend who threatens to damage his or her reputation. The two people have been friends, but the person wants to move up the social ladder at school and feels he or she can't do it and retain this particular friendship. (He or she might confront the friend with some fancy excuses to couch the blow, followed by subtle or not-so-subtle hints. When all else fails, the person will probably have to come right out with the truth. But any and all other options kids think of should be encouraged.)

• Someone likes another person very much and wants to be asked out by the other person; but the other person has shown no interest. (Options might include the old "I'll have one of my friends talk to one of his or her friends" routine, the direct approach, stalking the other person around the halls and neighborhoods, etc.)

After the skits have been performed, ask: **Do any of these things remind you of things you've done in the past?**

Why do you think we sometimes become so desperate to impress certain people or achieve certain goals—especially

at school?

What's the most embarrassing thing you've ever done to try to accomplish a goal similar to the ones we've acted out? What were the results of your actions? Get responses from several of your group members for each question.

A New Kid in Town

Ask a volunteer to stand in front of the rest of the group. Say: **This person has just moved to this area and will be going to your school. He** (or **she**) **knows nothing about the school, the teachers, the traditions, or anything else. What advice would you give him** (or **her**) **to help him** (or **her**) **fit in as quickly as possible?**

Let each person offer a nugget of advice. If group members have trouble coming up with ideas, you might want to have them identify who the "lousy" teachers are at school (and how to deal with them), which groups and organizations all the "cool" people belong to (and which ones are for the "losers"), what he or she needs to know about avoiding trouble with bullies, where to sit in the cafeteria, and so forth.

Try to make group members comfortable enough to be completely honest. Then, after no one has any further helpful hints, say: **Oh, by the way, this person's name is Jesus. He has some big plans when He grows up, but first He has to get through junior high and high school.**

Would any of your group members be a bit embarrassed or uncomfortable to have told a young Jesus some of the things they did? Explain that sometimes we have one set of standards that we discuss and display at church, but those things never quite make it to the hallways at school. It's very difficult to live out what we say we believe in a pressure-packed situation like school. Yet it is important that we begin to do so, or at least make a good attempt.

STEP 3

Cause for Concern?

(Needed: Copies of Repro Resource 3, pencils)

Have group members continue thinking about how Jesus might fit in as a student at their school(s) as you hand out copies of "Checkin' Out the School Scene" (Repro Resource 3) and pencils. Group members will be asked to estimate Jesus' level of comfort in a number of different situations He might experience on an average school day. They will then compare that degree of comfort in each category with their own comfort level.

Group members may discover that they have learned to take for granted or to dismiss certain activities that *should* be cause for concern. If so, try to let them struggle with these discoveries on their own. Resist any inclination to suggest what they should think about peers who choose to cheat, manipulate, and so forth. It is important that young people learn to monitor *their own* actions and attitudes. As they do, they will then become better able to deal with *others* who may not agree with them. Later in the session, group members will have the opportunity to think more about their attitudes and set some goals for themselves.

After everyone has completed the sheet, ask: **Do you think Jesus would like school? Why or why not?**

What do you think He would like most? What would He like least?

How do you think Jesus would dress for school?

Who would be His closest friends? Which groups would He belong to?

What would be in His locker? How might His locker be decorated?

It may be difficult for group members to envision Jesus as a junior high student. We know very little about His childhood, yet your group members need to be reminded that at one time He was indeed a young teen. And only by trying to see how He might have fit in at school can your kids see how *they* ought to try to fit in and what changes they might need to make in their attitudes or behavior.

STEP 4

Rabbi's Pet?

(Needed: Bibles, copies of Repro Resource 4, pencils)

Ask: **If you could ditch your parents for three days—let's say they have to go off on a trip while you stay home—and you could do anything you wanted without getting caught, what might you do?** Let group members speculate about their actions. Some might attempt wild kinds of things. Most would probably not try anything too ambitious.

What do you think Jesus might do under the same conditions? Get a few responses.

Explain to your group members that we do have one good look at Jesus as a young teen, and that single peek suggests an answer to the previous question. Have someone read Luke 2:41-52. Then explain that the synagogue at this time was not simply a place to worship once a week. It was also a center of teaching and learning—a place of schooling in addition to worship. Knowledgeable visitors would frequently be invited to teach, and attenders had the opportunity to learn from a number of people.

Ask: **What do you find most unusual about this story?** Get a few responses.

Do you think Jesus was too young to be hobnobbing with the religious teachers? (In this culture, age thirteen was the accepted time for males to begin to be accepted as adults. So at age twelve, it was not so unusual for them to be preparing for their "official" acceptance into society.)

If you suddenly dropped into the teachers' lounge at school and began a deep discussion about the things you were being taught, who in the group do you think would be most surprised? Why?

Why do you think Jesus stayed in Jerusalem—in school—instead of going with His parents? Do you think He was wrong in staying? Why?

Do you think Jesus was a young show-off with a "know-it-all" attitude? Explain. (It doesn't appear so. We read that He was "listening to them and asking them questions" [vs. 46].)

On a scale of one to ten—with ten being the highest—how well would you say you listen during most of your classes? How frequently do you take enough interest to ask questions

about the things you've heard?

Do you think Jesus knew things without having to study, or did He need to learn just like everyone else? (Verse 52 tells us He "grew in wisdom," so it appears that—though He was divine—He learned in much the same way that other young teens of His time learned.)

Do you think there's a difference in the kind of learning Jesus was doing in the synagogue and the kind of learning you do in school? If so, what is it? If no one mentions it, point out that in church settings we tend to place a higher value on spiritual learning than on, say, geometry. Yet if we truly believe that all truth is God's truth, *everything* we learn can help make us better Christians. Perhaps if we looked harder to find reflections of God at school—in the unchanging logic of geometry, the fascinating workings of the body in biology, the annals of history, and so forth—classes would be less of a drudgery for many people.

Hand out copies of "Jesus and Me" (Repro Resource 4). Whereas Repro Resource 3 had kids compare their responses to Jesus' expected response in a number of school-related settings, this one asks them to focus more on spiritual areas. Have them compare their own commitment toward spiritual learning to that of Jesus when He was approximately their age. The sheet should follow up your group discussion with some personal considerations. When everyone finishes, let volunteers share some of the observations they made about themselves.

STEP
5

Don't Know Much about Servanthood

(Needed: Bibles, paper, pencils)

Ask: **When you think about an average day at school, what three adjectives come to mind?** Encourage honest responses.

What words would you use to describe your *attitude* toward school? Some kids may truly enjoy the learning aspects of school. Others may focus primarily on the social opportunities. A few group members may have little interest in anything school has to offer.

If getting ahead at school were more important than anything else to you—if you wanted to make straight A's, be accepted by all of the cool people, and get involved in all of the extracurricular activities you enjoy—what would you

need to do differently than you're doing now? Let kids respond.

Should this be a goal for us—to get ahead no matter what?

After some discussion, explain: **Jesus' disciples had similar concerns about which one was the greatest** (Luke 22:24)**, and—as you're about to see—one of their mothers even got involved in trying to convince Jesus to let her sons be His number one and number two students. Jesus had to "referee" to keep His disciples from getting too far off track. It wasn't that He didn't want them to excel. But He wanted to make it clear that there were things more important than straight A's, awards, and other public recognition.**

Have someone read Matthew 20:20-28. Then say: **These verses are usually used in reference to spiritual growth. How might they apply to your life *at school*?**

After some discussion, hand out paper and pencils. Ask group members to make two columns on the paper. As they think about Jesus' command to be servants, they should list in the first column, "Things I need to *start* doing in order to be a better servant at school." The second column should contain a list of "Things I need to *stop* doing in order to be a better servant at school." After giving group members some time to make their lists, let volunteers share their responses.

Then ask: **What are some ways you could be a "servant" or a "slave" to other people at school? Of these things that you've listed, which ones might you actually be willing to try? Which ones do you feel are simply asking too much of you?**

Think back to some of the skits at the beginning of this session. In the context of these verses, how do you think Jesus would feel about your cheating on tests in order to get into a better college? How about breaking off relationships merely to move up the social ladder? Get several responses.

Why should we be willing to serve other people at school when they don't care for us or even acknowledge that we exist? (Some things we ought to do because we know they're right actions and not necessarily because we're getting anything out of them. As Christians, we can do our best to be better friends to each other without getting caught in the get-ahead-at-any-cost mentality.)

As you close, challenge your group members with a mental assignment for the next time they return to school. Ask them to go through as much of the day as possible attempting to see everything as if Jesus were observing it. They should try to become more aware of overheard conversations, rest room graffiti, social and ethnic divisions, and so forth. In addition, they should see *themselves* from a different perspective. Their comments, relationships, behavior toward authority, and everything else should be examined. It's fairly common to speak of Jesus being with us all the time and knowing all about us, but it can be quite an eye-opening experience to imagine Him actually walking school halls and getting a firsthand view of what's going on.

Step 3

You can convert Repro Resource 3 into a more active exercise by assigning parts and letting kids act out several of the situations, rather than simply having them fill out the sheet. One person can play the role of the young Jesus and another can play the role of the person showing Him around school. The pair should literally walk around the room, where other group members are playing the roles of students who are doing things like copying homework, harassing others, snubbing people at the lunch table, and so forth. At each confrontation, "freeze" the action and let group members determine how uncomfortable they think they might be if they were with Jesus at that particular moment in real life. Then move on to the next setting.

Step 5

After the discussion about serving other people at school, have kids form groups. Instruct each group to write and choreograph a few servanthood cheers—catchy and enthusiastic challenges that will help kids remember that they need to put other people first. (For example: "We're number two! We're number two! We serve you, so we're number two!") Give the groups a few minutes to practice their arm motions and choreography before they present their cheers to everyone else. Many group members will probably be familiar with actual cheers they can imitate, but even those who don't should be able to come up with some good ones anyway.

Step 1

Rather than opening the session with the skits as written (which would require having the same people perform a number of them), begin instead with a complete-the-sentence activity. Begin a number of sentences (one at a time) and then have each group member complete them. The sentences should be school-related, and might include the following:

• **The hardest thing about school is . . .**
• **I feel most alone at school when . . .**
• **The thing everyone seems to be good at in school except me is . . .**
• **If I could change one thing about school, it would be . . .**
• **When it comes to grades, I think . . .**

Step 5

Have your group members make "servanthood commitments" to each other. Distribute paper and pencils. Instruct kids to create three vertical columns across the top of the sheet: "Name," "Act of Service," and "Date/Time." Under the "Name" column, have them list the names of all the other group members. Then challenge each person to commit to performing an act of service for everyone else in the group. The acts of service should be done sometime during the following week—not immediately, or the tendency will be to do small things to "get it over with." (This activity should require some serious thought.) When group members complete an act of service, they should record it in the second column as well as listing the date and time in the third column. Explain that some of the best acts of service are things that are done anonymously, such as sending "Secret Pal" cards or gifts, doing a dreaded chore for someone when he or she isn't looking, etc. Follow up next week to see if everyone has fulfilled his or her commitments.

Step 3

Follow up the "Jesus comes to your school" concept by taking an "official poll." Ask a number of questions and then determine the percentage of people who respond with a yes, no, or "undecided." Here are some questions you might use:
• **Would you walk up to and welcome a Jewish stranger on his first day at your school?**
• **If a new kid seemed to be lost, would you volunteer to help?**
• **Would you make jokes about a stranger to your "regular" friends?**
• **Would you be jealous of a new kid who seemed to be smarter and/or nicer than you were?**

Encourage your group members to be honest about how they would respond to a *normal* stranger. Obviously, if they knew the person was Jesus, they would be more likely to treat Him kindly. But the challenge is to learn to treat *everyone* kindly.

Step 5

Learning to be a servant to others (especially at school) is a difficult thing to do—partially because young people may not tend to think about Christian living when they get into the "rhythm" of an average day at school. To help group members remember the importance of carrying their faith into their school hallways, create something as a group that kids can wear on a specified day or week. You might want to come up with a T-shirt design, make buttons, cut cloth swatches or ribbons, or use any number of other methods. But if you have a large group, and everyone agrees to wear something symbolic to help him or her remember to be a servant in school, kids won't have the excuse of "spiritual amnesia." In addition, as kids at school question why so many others are wearing the same symbol, your group members can explain that it's to help remind them to invite new people to your youth group or Sunday school (which certainly qualifies as helping to "serve" people).

Step 2

Sometimes it helps to address a "heard it all before" mentality by making some rapid about-turns in your teaching. So after your group members get into the Jesus-as-fellow-student concept, suddenly shift the discussion. Say: **Suppose Jesus were one of your *teachers*. Do you think that would be a good thing or a bad thing? Why?** Let group members respond. If you wish, have kids act out a scene in which Jesus is trying to teach a class of rowdy students. Try to help group members see that in reality, Jesus serves both as our friend and our teacher. We need to learn to relate to Him on both levels and, based on His example, learn to relate better to other people as well.

Step 4

If your kids are occasionally difficult to teach due to a know-it-all attitude, spend some time immediately after reading Luke 2:41-52 in a discussion of Jesus' attitude as described in this passage. Ask: **What attitude should we have toward parents and teachers—even if we might know more than they do?** (We should be submissive and obedient.) **Why do you think Jesus was submissive to His parents, even though they didn't understand Him?** (If children don't submit to parents, there is little, if any, order within a family. Besides, a child's submission usually reduces conflict within the family and gives parents the opportunity to change their minds and apologize if they are wrong.) **If you were to follow Jesus' example at school, what are some things you might need to do differently?** (Be less argumentative when disagreeing with a teacher? Be patient in asking questions? Learn without being so self-assured that you already know it all?) Point out that if anyone had the right to claim, "I've heard it all before," it was Jesus, who left heaven to come to earth. But if even *He* didn't give His teachers a hard time (at least, not when He was twelve), then neither should anyone else.

Step 2

For people unfamiliar with the Bible, the concept of Jesus as a junior higher may be hard to grasp. They may be dealing with artistic portrayals filed away in their minds—pictures of a rather weak-looking adult who doesn't look very happy. It may be difficult for them to think of Jesus as a happy and active teenager. So spend a little time helping your kids make that mental shift. Say: **Think of the things you've done at school and at school-related functions during the past week. Which of those things do you think Jesus would really have enjoyed? Which do you think He might have avoided? Why?** Keep asking questions to try to show that Jesus was fully human. He felt many of the identical emotions and feelings that we have every day. Only by relating to His human experiences can we fully appreciate His divine function in our ultimate forgiveness and salvation.

Step 5

When you get to the end of the session, don't downplay the importance of applying what has been learned. Just because your kids may not know much about the Bible doesn't mean they can't put into practice what they *do* know. So focus on the importance of servanthood with a skit. Simulate a restaurant setting in which three or four people are seated. Another person should approach and say, "Hello. My name is _____. I'll be your server this evening. What can I do for you?" The seated kids should answer honestly by listing needs they have. The server may or may not be able to help, but should try to do whatever he or she can do to accommodate the requests. Afterward, discuss how service need not be a negative or inconvenient concept. Willing servants learn to genuinely enjoy what they do for other people. After several of your group members have had the opportunity to "practice" on each other, challenge them to become more servant-minded toward other people at school.

Step 2

At the end of Step 2, after challenging group members to live out their faith at school, continue the discussion by having kids analyze some of their friendships. Ask: **What do friends do that bring them closer together? What are the qualities and characteristics that you look for in a friend? Which of these attributes do you feel are most important?** Group members should come up with a list of elements of friendship that includes qualities such as good communication, shared interests, time spent together, forgiveness, patience, and so forth. After they do, go back through the list and discuss how each of these characteristics might apply to a relationship with Jesus. Can a relationship with Him grow stronger if we don't spend time, share what's on our minds, ask for help when we need it, and so forth? If group members can begin to perceive Jesus as a close friend rather than a remote force of the universe, their fellowship with each other will become stronger and their worship of Him will be more heartfelt and effective.

Step 4

When Jesus was in the temple with the religious leaders, He was not only "listening to them," but He also had the opportunity for "asking them questions." Many young people have little, if any, opportunity to converse with church leaders one on one. If this is true for your group members, plan to have your pastor sit in on this session. Or you may want to plan a separate session in which group members can ask the pastor anything. Most young people are likely to have questions in mind—if not their own, perhaps of some of the things they are asked by non-Christian kids at school. If they are slow getting started with their own questions, begin with a few of your own ("Where did the Bible come from and how do we know it's the Word of God?" "What do you tell someone who asks you what we believe at our church?").

Step 1

For your group of mostly girls, you might want to add the following scenario to the skit choices at the beginning of the session:
• Someone is the only girl in the entire junior high school who doesn't wear makeup. Her parents have said she must wait until she's in high school. (She might keep makeup hidden and put it on when she gets to school, openly defy her parents and wear it anyway, try to sneak it past her parents, etc.)

Step 2

If there are no guys in your group, you might want to ask a male from your church to make a guest appearance to portray Jesus. If possible, you could use a guy from another Sunday school class or someone your group members don't know at all. If you can't find a male recruit, ask one of your girls to portray Jesus. Give her some "male" props (such as a baseball cap) to use during the activity. No matter who you use for the roleplay, make sure you suggest to the group that this new student is a bit "different." Afterward, you can talk about how group members' advice would or wouldn't differ according to whether they thought the new person was a "loser" or not.

Step 3

In the discussion about what Jesus might have been like, encourage your guys to speculate on the "toughness" of Jesus. Ask: **If Jesus were your age and going to your school, do you think He would get beat up a lot? Would He try out for baseball, football, soccer, or other sports? If so, what position(s) would He play? Would He enjoy roughhousing with the guys? If we were to hold an arm-wrestling competition among ourselves, where do you think He would place?** Explain that Jesus was never a weakling as an adult, and there is no reason to believe He might have been as a child. Though some guys have a tendency to think of Christian living as somehow unmanly, Jesus was perhaps the strongest person who ever lived when we consider His willingness to die on the cross for our sins.

Step 4

Point out that Jesus was consistent in His behavior. He didn't seem to have one standard when His parents and teachers were around, and an entirely different one when they were absent. Can your guys make the same claim? Have a couple of group members create a number of skits in which someone walks up to his best friend and asks, "What did you do at the party this weekend?" The friend might admit that he checked out the girls, listened to some new rock CDs that were sexually suggestive, maybe had a drink or two, etc. After the conversation between friends, have someone playing your pastor walk up to the guy and ask exactly the same question. See how the person's answer varies. Other questions for additional skits might include the following: "How was your date with Jane the other night?" "What kind of trouble have you gotten into this week?" "Have you seen the latest *Sports Illustrated* swimsuit edition?"

Step 1

Begin the session by playing Seat Shuffle. Have everyone sit in chairs in a circle (facing inward)—except for one person, who stands in the center. There should be one empty chair in the circle. The goal of the center person is to sit down. But as he or she approaches the empty seat, other group members should shift to that seat to try to prevent the person from sitting. This, of course, opens other seats. So the center person continues to try to fit in somewhere. When he or she finally lunges into an empty seat, the person to his or her right goes to the center. The game can demonstrate how difficult it is to "break in" to certain groups at school or elsewhere. Explain that even though it may be difficult to make honor clubs, sports teams, or other worthwhile groups, it is usually worth the effort. Even if we don't eventually make it, the struggle to get there can be beneficial.

Step 5

You can make the application exercise more fun by adding a number of comic possibilities. For example, you might hand out index cards and pencils and ask kids to list the following:
(1) A word to describe their cafeteria food
(2) A nickname they might give their least liked teacher
(3) A word to describe the smell of their locker
(4) Something specific they plan to do this week to be better servants of others at school

Collect the cards and see how well group members can guess who wrote what. Pay special attention to the intended acts of service, but have fun with the rest.

Step 2

If Jesus actually showed up at your group members' school(s), what kind of attention might it generate? Have kids form small groups. Instruct the members of each group to work together to write headlines and lead sentences for the school newspaper's coverage of Jesus' visit. As time permits, they can also work on the rest of the article. But their primary focus should be to craft a headline that will capture people's attention, followed by a lead sentence that would provide information and generate excitement about Jesus' unexpected appearance at school. Give the groups a few minutes to work. When everyone is finished, have each group share what it came up with.

Step 3

Another thing kids would need to think about if Jesus were going to their school (as a fellow junior higher) would be what to write in His yearbook. Once a year, no medium is more important to young people than the yearbook. Ask: **How many times do you think Jesus' picture would be in the yearbook? What clubs would He belong to? In the candid shots, what do you think He would be doing?** After the discussion, pass around pieces of paper. Have each group member write down (1) what he or she would write in Jesus' yearbook, and (2) what he or she thinks Jesus might write (in return) at the end of a year spent together. Read group members' comments and see if they're beginning to get a sense of what Jesus might have been like as a junior higher.

Step 2

Combine Steps 1 and 2 with the following activity. Explain that there's a kid who is hurriedly getting ready for his first day of junior high. He could really use some advice about what to do, what not to do, whom to hang out with, which teachers to avoid, etc. Unfortunately, he doesn't have time to stand around and talk; he has to catch the bus. So each of your group members should write this person a brief note that he can read on the bus, giving him some advice to alleviate the pressure of the first day of school. After a few minutes, ask volunteers to read their notes. Then announce that the new kid is Jesus. See if any kids would change their advice, knowing now who they're advising. Then move on to Step 3.

Step 4

Skip Step 4; use the passage in Step 5 (Matthew 20:20-28) for your Bible study. To help kids understand what it means to be a "servant" at school, name some everyday school situations and let kids tell you what a servant's response would be. Here are some situations you could use:
• **One of your friends asks you to help him study for an upcoming history test. Usually when you study with this person, you spend so much time answering his questions that you don't get to study for yourself. The history test is two days away. If you help your friend study, you may not have enough time to prepare for the test yourself.**
• **Inga, the new transfer student from Sweden, asks you to sit with her at lunch. You're uncomfortable around Inga because you have a hard time understanding her when she speaks. You try to get some of your other friends to accompany you, but they refuse. They tease you about how boring your lunch with Inga is going to be and make plans to sit at a nearby table to make faces at you behind Inga's back.**

Step 2

For many urban kids who live in tough neighborhoods, simply getting to and from school is difficult. Add this fact to the "new kid" scenario. Ask your group members what advice they would give the new kid about getting to and from school safely. Some group members may suggest that the new kid get involved in extracurricular activities to avoid being out on the streets right after school. Others might suggest taking a bus or cab to school, if possible. Still others may suggest joining a gang for "protection." After you reveal that the new kid is Jesus, see how many of your group members would change their advice.

Step 3

Bring in a wide array of clothing styles that one might find at a typical urban junior high school. (If such clothes aren't hanging in your closet, you may want to ask your group members to bring them in.) Place these clothes at the front of the room. Have kids form groups. Assign each group a particular "clique" or social group found in most urban junior high schools—jocks, computer geeks, burnouts, future "yuppies" or "buppies," etc. Instruct each group to come to the front of the room one at a time to choose the clothes that a person would have to wear to fit into its assigned social group. Afterward, discuss the importance of having the "right" clothes when it comes to fitting in at school.

Step 1

When you form teams and assign skit topics, make sure you have at least one team of junior highers and one team of high schoolers. Instruct the teams to plan a skit in which a person's goal is to impress members of the other team. For example, the junior high team should act out the things a junior higher would do to try to capture the high schoolers' attention and admiration. The high school group, on the other hand, should try to come up with things they think junior highers would respond to. From the actions included in the skits, you should see how your kids perceive each other. After the skits have been performed, ask: **Which of the things illustrated by the other team did you find most effective? Which things wouldn't have worked on you at all? Do you find yourself ever trying to impress people who are older or younger than you? Why?**

Step 4

After you read the story of Jesus in the temple, discuss what impact this twelve year old might have had on the "older and wiser" religious leaders. We know that the people in the temple were "amazed at His understanding and His answers," but we don't know exactly what they were thinking. Speculate about this. Have one of your youngest guys represent Jesus. Place him in the center of the room. Have everyone else suppose that he has just finished explaining to them exactly how the message of the minor prophets is relevant to young people today. Point out that besides his vast spiritual knowledge, the person is absolutely normal. Have other kids express what they would be thinking if this actually happened. Then discuss how the crowd of religious teachers must have felt as they witnessed such wisdom from a twelve year old. Challenge kids not to be intimidated by older people if they have something to say. They should contribute their own God-given wisdom in appropriate ways, regardless of the setting.

Step 1

Begin the session very formally, as if it were a school classroom. (Or you might want to create an excuse to be absent and have another adult "fill in" for you. Your replacement should be very "proper" in demeanor and presentation of material.) Watch the responses of group members. How do they respond to a setting that is very much like school? Is it with dread? Rebellion? Enjoyment? Follow up with a verbal discussion of how they were feeling. Ask: **What things do we do in this group that you enjoy more than school? What are some things you do at school that might make this group more fun? What are the best emotions you feel at school? What are the worst?** It shouldn't take long to discover a lot about your group members' attitude toward school before going on with the rest of the session.

Step 3

Repro Resource 3 may not apply as well to sixth graders as it does to older kids. Rather than make copies of the sheet and hand it out, you might want to pick and choose the activities on the sheet you want your kids to deal with (and add other situations of your own). One of the simplest ways to have group members respond is to read each statement and have everyone simultaneously hold up a number of fingers between 1 and 10 to indicate his or her level of comfort in that particular instance. Encourage people at either extreme of the scale to explain why they feel so strongly. It won't take long to go through the sheet with this method, and you can still cover much of the same material without dealing with things you don't feel group members are yet ready for.

Date Used:

Approx. Time

Step 1: Whatever It Takes _____
o Small Group
o Mostly Girls
o Extra Fun
o Combined Jr. High/High School
o Sixth Grade

Step 2: A New Kid in Town _____
o Heard It All Before
o Little Bible Background
o Fellowship & Worship
o Mostly Girls
o Media
o Short Meeting Time
o Urban

Step 3: Cause for Concern? _____
o Extra Action
o Large Group
o Mostly Guys
o Media
o Urban
o Sixth Grade

Step 4: Rabbi's Pet? _____
o Heard It All Before
o Fellowship & Worship
o Mostly Guys
o Short Meeting Time
o Combined Jr. High/High School

Step 5: Don't Know Much About Servanthood _____
o Extra Action
o Small Group
o Large Group
o Little Bible Background
o Extra Fun

3 ... What Would Jesus Do in My Church?

YOUR GOALS FOR THIS SESSION:

Choose one or more

☐ To help kids see that much of their behavior at church may not reflect the intended goals of worship or of building a sense of community.

☐ To help kids understand that they are indeed valuable members of the body of Christ and should assume more ownership of what takes place during the church service.

☐ To help kids learn to tolerate the parts of the church service they find boring or nonproductive and to help them establish a stronger one-on-one relationship with Jesus as they do.

☐ Other _____
_____

Your Bible Base:

Matthew 6:1-18
Luke 4:14-30
John 2:12-16

Praying Attention

(Needed: Copies of Repro Resource 5, pencils)

Call for volunteers, one pair at a time. Each pair should conduct a "conversation" in which each person talks only about one of his or her concerns while neglecting to listen to the other person. For example, one person might talk about Friday night's game while the other talks about problems with her parents. The participants should take turns speaking, as in a conversation, yet not give any indication of hearing or responding to the other. See how long your volunteers can go without acknowledging what each other is saying. To add a twist to the activity, you might instruct the members of one pair to converse without using the word *I*. Then you might have the members of another pair use the word *I* in every sentence they speak.

Afterward, explain that these conversations model some of our attempts at worship and prayer. Sometimes we pour out everything we want Jesus to do for us, and He tries to answer; but because we haven't trained ourselves to listen, we can't hear Him. We just keep talking. Other times we may focus entirely on ourselves, or go to the other extreme and become so detached from the act of worship that we'd do just as well not to be there.

Hand out copies of "No-Point Bulletin" (Repro Resource 5) and pencils. Challenge group members to be honest as they describe what they *actually* do during certain segments of a worship service.

When everyone is finished, ask: **Do you find your mind wondering during church services pretty often, or only every once in a while?**

Why do you think it's sometimes so difficult to stay focused on what's going on in the church service?

On a scale of one to ten—with ten being the worst—how bad do you think it is to sit through a church worship service without really paying attention to what's going on? Why? Get several responses to each of these questions.

STEP
2

The Problem with Church

If group members seem tentative or reluctant to come right out and say that sometimes the church worship service just isn't exciting enough to hold their attention, have them respond to the following agree/ disagree statements. Designate one wall as "Totally agree" and the opposite wall as "Totally disagree." Then read one statement at a time and let group members stand at the appropriate place in the room to show to what extent they agree with it. Here are some suggestions to get you started:

• **If people don't get something out of the church service, it indicates a spiritual problem on their part.**

• **People should leave every worship service feeling spiritually challenged, fulfilled, and excited.**

• **To be absolutely truthful, I find church boring much of the time.**

• **I would probably get more out of worship if I went off by myself and worshiped God on my own.**

• **Our church service is mostly for older people, not for people my age.**

• **The sermons are usually too long and formal.**

• **The music couldn't be any better.**

• **If I were in charge of the worship service, things would be a lot different.**

Some young people may be surprised to discover that not every older person is completely happy with the structure and format of corporate worship. You might want to be honest about any changes *you* would like to see, or describe alternative types of activities you've witnessed in other churches.

Then ask: **When people don't like the format of a church service, is their best option to leave and find another church? Explain.** If no one mentions it, suggest that finding another church might be the final answer, but it shouldn't be the first one. People need to express their opinions courteously to the appropriate leaders in the church—the pastor, board members, and so forth.

What can you do if you would like to see things done differently? It is fairly common to hear young people complain about how boring church is, but we may need to pay more attention to their comments. Such remarks show that they are involved and desire to see

OPTIONS

EXTRA ACTION

SMALL GROUP

HEARD IT ALL BEFORE

FELLOWSHIP & WORSHIP

MOSTLY GUYS

EXTRA FUN

SHORT MEETING TIME

URBAN

things change for the better. Help kids discover what steps they could take to suggest changes in your specific church. Might they volunteer to lead a service and teach some livelier songs to the congregation? Could representatives attend a board meeting or congregational meeting to express the feelings of the young people?

STEP 3

Rebel with a Cause

(Needed: Bibles)

Ask: **If Jesus walked into our church and sat through the worship service one day, do you think He would want to see any changes made in the format? If so, what? Or do you think His primary concern would be in the responses and attitudes of the people in the congregation?** The first response of your young people might be that Jesus would note their lack of attention and want them to stop whining about the tempo of the songs and the length of the sermon. More than likely, they assume you're going to tell them to improve their attitudes. And while that might be a good idea, it is also important for them to see that even Jesus didn't always fit in during established, formal worship services.

Before you get into the actual Bible study in Step 4, have volunteers look up and read Luke 4:14-30 and John 2:12-16. Explain (somewhat tongue in cheek): **Since we look to Jesus as a model for how to live in almost every area of life, we should surely find good help for how to act in response to religious teaching and church life. These days we worship Jesus, but let's see what kind of worshiper Jesus was.**

Have your first volunteer read Luke 4:14-30. In this passage, group members should discover that

• Jesus took an active part in the worship services He attended, teaching in many places.

• Jesus was a good teacher. ("Everyone praised him" [vs. 15].)

• When He got to His hometown of Nazareth, He was not perceived so much as "Jesus, the great teacher," but rather "Jesus, Joe's kid."

• Jesus spoke the absolute truth even when He knew it might irritate His listeners. He didn't simply tell people what they wanted to hear.

• His "friends and neighbors" became so irate with Him that they tried to toss Him off a cliff.

Have your second volunteer read John 2:12-16. In this passage, group members should discover that

• Jesus worshiped not only on the sabbath, but also took part in special religious celebrations like the Passover.

• When He saw things He didn't like, He took action to do something about them.

• In extreme circumstances, His actions were immediate and severe.

• His anger was not due to His personal dissatisfaction with the worship, but rather that God's house was being treated with extreme disrespect.

Ask: **Are these our two best options for improving the church service: to speak our minds and risk death at the hands of fellow congregation members, or to pick up a whip and physically change the things we don't like? If not, what can we learn from these two examples of Jesus?** Point out that in both cases, Jesus displayed a desire for change. In one case, He was extremely vulnerable; in the other, He was extremely bold. It would appear that there is no single correct way to respond to the things we are dissatisfied with in our worship services. Our behavior should depend largely on the good or bad things that are taking place. We also need to remember that Jesus was a knowledgeable teacher who knew for sure what was right and wrong. Most young people are still in the learning stages. So they may not be justified in taking the exact same action that Jesus displayed.

Ask: **If you are powerless to change things you don't like or don't agree with in the worship service, what can you do?** Get a few responses.

STEP
4

It's a Secret

(Needed: Bibles)

Have kids form three groups. Assign each group a short section of Matthew 6 to read and discuss:

Group #1—Matthew 6:1-4

Group #2—Matthew 6:5-15

Group #3—Matthew 6:16-18

Explain that this portion of Scripture is part of Jesus' famous Sermon on the Mount. In this section He is dealing with right and wrong ways to

OPTIONS

LARGE GROUP

LITTLE BIBLE BACKGROUND

FELLOWSHIP & WORSHIP

MOSTLY GIRLS

JR. HIGH / HIGH SCHOOL COMBINED

worship. Ask each group to explain and/or demonstrate a right way and a wrong way to worship God, based on its assigned passage.

Group #1 should discuss the issue of giving. The wrong way to give to the needy is to make a big deal about it. Jesus describes trumpets being blown to announce giving by hypocritical men. Today some churches have other means of honoring major donors to the church. But Jesus says these people have their reward. God Himself rewards giving done in secret.

Group #2 will discuss the topic of prayer. Some people seem to enjoy praying "for show." Jesus tells us to pray on our own to God the Father. He also tells us that the quantity of our words is not nearly as important as the quality of what we're saying. Prayer should also be accompanied by action. As we ask God to forgive the things we've done wrong, we need to forgive people who've done things to offend us.

Group #3 has the shortest, but most challenging, of the passages. Since fasting is not a widespread church discipline these days, you might want to have group members think in terms of "suffering for the Lord." Sometimes people make a big deal about the sacrifices they make to be a good Christian. The principles concerning fasting can apply in such cases. If we're truly doing these things for God, we shouldn't complain or try to get other Christians to give us a pity party. Rather, we should show how much we're enjoying ourselves as we devote ourselves more completely to Him.

Say: **It's unrealistic to expect everything in a public worship service to conform exactly to the way we want it. Probably no church you attend will do everything to perfectly suit your mood every single Sunday. Much of what we get out of any church service has to do with what we put into it. And in extreme cases, you may find that the church is way off track and that you need to go somewhere else.** (Most congregations frown on young teens storming down the aisles with whips. These days we have many more options than worshipers during Jesus' time.)

But one thing Jesus tells us in the Sermon on the Mount is that *the secret to worship is secret worship*. We shouldn't expect to have all of our needs met in a public church service. The church is comprised of many different kinds of people and personalities. It should be clear that not *everyone* will be completely satisfied with what goes on for one hour on Sunday morning. So Jesus tells us that our needs will be attended to during our regular personal times with God. If Jesus Himself didn't fit into a traditional worship service, we can expect to find ourselves feeling out of place from time to time. But Jesus didn't walk away and give up, and we shouldn't either. We should follow His example and try to make improvements where we can, all the while keeping our personal relationship with Him strong.

STEP 5

Consultant Results

(Needed: Copies of Repro Resource 6, pencils)

Explain that sometimes churches spend large amounts of money to bring in consultants who will sit through several worship services and make recommendations for changes that will improve the quality of the worship. Designate your group members to be a consultant group and give them the same assignment. Hand out copies of "Any Ideas?" (Repro Resource 6), which will provide them with some things they need to consider in their evaluations. As time permits, try to tailor the sheet for your own worship service. Brainstorm specific goals to add to those already on the sheet. Each church is different, and the more specific you can be as to what group members should look for, the more they should get out of this exercise.

You might also want to have group members predict what they will discover during the church service, and later compare their expectations with what they actually discover. It's not unusual to focus so much on the few things we dislike about church that we miss out on all of the good things that take place. When young people take a fresh and objective look at the worship service, the church frequently looks like a much more promising place than they had originally thought.

Emphasize that group members should make evaluations based not on personal preferences, but on whether or not Jesus would be pleased with what's going on. The focus of a worship service should be Christ. When this is true, the good feelings of the participants usually become an automatic by-product.

Close with a challenge for your group members to work on any lax personal worship habits they might have developed. Encourage them to eliminate any signs of hypocrisy or other sinful attitudes from their own lives—and not to be so critical of others. Finally, offer praise in a closing prayer, asking Jesus to provide the insight to allow all group members (and leaders) to keep Him preeminent in their personal and corporate spiritual lives.

OPTIONS

SMALL GROUP

LARGE GROUP

EXTRA FUN

MEDIA

SHORT MEETING TIME

URBAN

JR. HIGH / HIGH SCHOOL COMBINED

SIXTH GRADE

No-Point Bulletin

Believe it or not, a lot of thought goes into the structure of most church services. The pastor chooses the sermon topic and delivers it with much concern for the message. Hymns and other musical choices are made by someone—deliberately and with a lot of care. Offerings, prayers, and other aspects of the worship service are all planned to have a desired effect on the worshiper. So how do you think all of those planners feel when people come to church and talk or sleep through the whole service?

Below is a bulletin from an average Sunday at First Typical Church. You see what is planned, and the *intent* of each activity. But be honest in describing what you *really* do during each of these activities. Your list might include daydreaming, concentrating on what's being said, gum chewing, homework, note passing, and so forth.

PRELUDE (Instrumental music to prepare people's hearts and minds for worship)

DOXOLOGY (Singing "Praise God from whom all blessings flow . . ." helps us take our minds off of ourselves and focus our thoughts, together, on God.)

HYMNS (Sung to express joy and praise to God)

SPECIAL MUSIC/TESTIMONY (An opportunity for individuals to share spiritual blessings with the entire congregation)

OFFERING (The privilege of giving back to God a portion of what He has provided for us)

PASTORAL PRAYER (The pastor takes the needs of the congregation to the Lord in prayer and asks God for His blessing on the service.)

SERMON (The pastor helps make God's Word more relevant to us.)

CLOSING SONG (A final opportunity to send everyone away joyful and praising God)

BENEDICTION (A request for God's ongoing blessing on His people during the next week)

Any Ideas?

Let's suppose you've never attended your church before in your life, and you're going for the first time. In addition, let's say that someone is paying you to evaluate the worship service and make recommendations for things that might need to be changed and made better.

Your first assignment is to sit through a church worship service, paying close attention to everything that goes on. As you do, assign a rating to each of the following categories by placing an X in the appropriate box (E = Excellent; G = Good; F = Fair; N = Needs improvement). Then, for everything that isn't already "Excellent," make some recommendations for how you think it can be improved. Remember, you must witness a church service from a fresh and unbiased point of view before your results will be considered valid.

	E	G	F	N	RECOMMENDATIONS
OVERALL ENVIRONMENT *THE BUILDING ITSELF* (Does everything look clean? Are the seats comfortable? Is the lighting good?)					
PERSONAL ATMOSPHERE (Are you greeted as you enter the door? Do the people seem friendly?)					
THE WORSHIP SERVICE *MUSIC* (Does the music set the proper mood for worship? Is it varied or pretty much the same style and tempo?)					
SERMON (Is the Word of God presented clearly? Did you learn anything you can apply this week?)					
FELLOWSHIP (Do you feel like part of a larger "body"? Is there an opportunity for you to contribute anything?)					
MISCELLANEOUS ASPECTS (Does the sequence of worship activities make sense? Did the service go smoothly?)					
OTHER CONSIDERATIONS In the space below, list other things you want to consider for your specific church; then rate them as you did the items above.					

Step 1

Begin the session with some kind of keep-away game (perhaps "Monkey in the Middle"), in which one person stands between two other people and tries to intercept a ball they are passing back and forth. If he or she successfully intercepts the ball, the person who threw it goes to the middle. Since the goal of the game is to prevent one person from receiving something sent from another, it can demonstrate the fact that sometimes we may be responsible for keeping other people from receiving a message or benefit from God. As you go through the rest of the session, focus on how we can help others worship more effectively rather than standing in their way.

Step 2

As you begin to discuss problems with the church, take your group members to the sanctuary. When someone has a comment to make about some problem in the church or a suggested improvement, have him or her go to the appropriate place in the sanctuary and express his or her opinion. For example, if the person wants to say, "I think the preaching is too boring," he or she should go to the pulpit to make the statement. At that point, other group members should cheer or applaud at a level that will indicate their agreement with the statement. Give everyone who wishes to do so the opportunity to stand in an appropriate spot and state opinions about the church worship service as others reply with various levels of noise. Group members' comments will probably cover many of the agree/disagree statements listed in Step 2. If not, you can initiate a discussion on the points they neglect to mention.

Step 2

Sometimes a young person's perceptions about church are strong, but not necessarily accurate. He or she may feel out of place or vastly outnumbered by "old" people. To see how accurate your kids' perceptions are, it might be interesting to estimate the average age of the people who go to your church. Have kids call out the names of everyone they can think of who attends your church. Write the names on the board as kids supply them. When you have a fairly sizable list of names, go back through them and try to estimate each person's age. Then add up the ages and divide that total by the number of names on the list to get your average. In many cases, when you consider the youngsters as well as the adults, the average age of churchgoers may not be nearly as high as your kids think. If you can help kids realize that they aren't so far from the median age of churchgoers, they may be willing to get more involved and feel that they're part of the church now, rather than waiting to "grow up" and participate at some future point.

Step 5

Create a scenario in which a new disease of epidemic proportions has wiped out the entire world except for the people in your room. (Perhaps church potluck food was the only antidote to the disease.) Now that your kids are the future of the world, ask them how they plan to keep the church going. Would this be an important priority for them? What changes would they make as they set up *their* new church? Who will be responsible for making sure they continue to read and study the Bible? Who will lead the singing? Is anyone willing to take on the teaching and praying responsibilities? After some discussion, have kids consider that some day such responsibilities may indeed be theirs. The sooner they get involved and become more serious about contributing their talents and gifts to the church, the better prepared they will be when the opportunity eventually arises.

Step 4

When you get ready to discuss the importance of individual worship, be aware that sometimes the tendency of members of a large group is to let participation in the group replace devotion to a more structured church service and/or personal spiritual growth. You might want to check to see if this is true of your group members. Explain that you will read a number of statements. Group members should stand if they agree and sit if they disagree. Some of your statements might include the following:

• I think it's OK to miss church occasionally as long as I keep coming to this group. (Answers may depend on what group members define as "occasionally.")

• I think going to church is more important than coming to this group.

• I think spending time alone with God every day is more important than coming to this group once a week.

• I spend time alone with God every day.

Use other statements you know will capture the attention of your specific group of young people.

Step 5

As a follow-up to the discussion on the pros and cons of your own particular church service, you might want to set up groups to visit other churches in your area. First, have group members use Repro Resource 6 to evaluate your own church service. But then arrange to have them do the same thing in other churches. Many times young people have questions about what other denominations believe or how they worship. By forming groups to visit other churches and report back to the large group, kids will be able to answer a lot of their questions as well as get a better perspective on and appreciation for your church's own style of worship.

Step 2

Prior to the meeting, collect bulletins from a number of different churches in your area. Also bring a recent bulletin from your own church. Based only on the bulletins, have your kids rate the churches in order of best to worst. See where your own church fits in their estimation. Discuss what led kids to establish the ratings they chose. Then challenge some of their assumptions. For example, a church with a lot of youth activities scheduled for the week might have ranked high. If so, ask: **Would you be willing to spend twelve** (or however many) **hours every week participating in these activities as well as Sunday worship, Bible study, and so forth? What if this church had so many people the leaders didn't even know your name?** Try to help kids see that they may tend to contrast the best points of other churches with the weaknesses of your church. If your kids are prone to jumping to conclusions before thinking a matter all the way through, this exercise might help them see that the carpeting isn't always greener in churches on the other side of town. Their own church has many good points and much to offer them.

Step 3

After allowing kids to voice complaints about church in Step 2 and then considering what Jesus might think of your church in Step 3, try to make sure everyone has expressed his or her strongest dissatisfaction. Then have someone read I Corinthians 12:12, 26, 27. Have kids think in terms of the church as the body of Christ. Ask: **How do you think Jesus must feel when we complain about what He has called His "body"?** Point out that when we think of "church" as a building or a place to spend an hour on Sunday mornings, it's easy to find things to criticize. But if we shift our thinking to see it more as the body of Christ—of which each person is a valuable part—we may not be quite so quick to complain.

Step 3

If your kids have little Bible background, you'll need to be careful as you cover the story of Jesus driving the salespeople out of the temple. Most kids should be able to understand why Jesus would be so angry—as long as you're careful to explain it and allow them to ask questions. Try to create a modern-day equivalent of the problem caused by the moneylenders. Say: **Suppose that you're in church this Sunday and the pastor is trying to explain an important passage to the congregation. Everyone is eager to hear what he has to say. Suddenly, people start walking up and down the aisles shouting, "T-shirts! Get your Pastor Smith T-shirts right here! Best preacher in town. Show your support. Only $18.95." Others are selling hot dogs and soft drinks "to help you keep up your strength and your attention level." Even though they might give valid reasons for selling their merchandise, do you think these people should be allowed to continue?** Let kids respond.

Step 4

Kids with little Bible background are likely to need help both with understanding the reasons why personal daily devotions are important and how to get started. Be prepared to provide them with some help. You may be able to find good devotional books at a Christian bookstore. If not, have kids read through one of the Gospels. Break down the book into several short readings that can be studied a day at a time. The advantage of having kids focus on the same passages during their devotional time is that they can discuss what they're learning when they get together as a group. They can also ask questions, knowing that their confusion may be shared by others. Be careful to start slow and simple, and not to intimidate kids by challenging them to do too much. Once they get in the habit, they should begin to find their own pace for individual study.

Step 2

To increase the quality of your group members' corporate worship, you might want to plan a "pre-worship worship service" for Sunday morning. Arrange to meet together as a group just prior to the morning worship service. (Five or ten minutes should be plenty.) During this time when young people are so often running around, catching up on gossip, staking out the "best" seats in the back of the church, and so forth, have them instead focus on the upcoming worship service. Give group members the opportunity to volunteer to lead one-minute devotionals, pray, lead a praise chorus, or otherwise help everyone prepare to worship God more effectively during the following hour. If your kids become more expectant about getting something out of a worship service, the experience is much more likely to be beneficial for them.

Step 4

A group devoted to improving worship may want to spend more time than most on the basics in Matthew 6. Rather than simply mentioning the activities in order to identify needs for personal devotion, group members should also evaluate how well they are doing in the areas of (1) giving, (2) prayer, and (3) fasting. They should set goals in each of these areas that need improvement. While as junior highers they may not have great quantities of money, and doing without food for long periods of time is not healthy for them, they should still be able to come up with some ideas that will make their personal times of worship more fulfilling. And when worship becomes more satisfying on a personal level, it should also be more uplifting in group settings as well.

Step 1

After your girls have completed their "conversations," ask: **How did you feel when you were talking and you could tell the other person wasn't listening at all?** (Degraded, hurt, unvalued.) **How did it feel to see people not responding to each other?** (Frustrating.) **Have you ever been in a conversation like the ones we just heard? If so, how did you feel?** Use this discussion to introduce the topic of prayer.

Step 4

As a group, brainstorm a list of specific things your group members can do to keep their personal relationships with Christ strong. Ideas might include having a personal praise time using favorite Christian music, starting a Bible study before or after school, keeping a consistent prayer time, etc. Be prepared to give personal examples that may help your girls think of other creative ways to worship God on their own that they may not have considered.

Step 2

Guys who are actively involved in sports are probably familiar with awards ceremonies. Many junior highers have sat through such events that honor older athletes. Ask: **What if the church gave awards for achievement? What do you think some of the awards should be? Who in our church—or group—do you think might deserve to be recognized?** Group members should see that truly admirable qualities are things like humility, servanthood, and forgiveness. The whole concept of publicly awarding people for being humble may seem silly. Yet that is exactly the reason we need to be more alert to selfless acts by other people. They *aren't* getting awards for such qualities—at least, not while they're here on earth—so the least we can do is express appreciation for what others do for us and thank them every time we see them doing something selfless.

Step 3

The idea of Jesus as a religious "rebel" may be new to your guys (who may be rebels in a different sense). Ask: **Is it really OK to stand up against traditions when those traditions are not good ones? Is it always right to do so, or would you say there are guidelines we should follow? What are some of those guidelines?** Many junior high guys tend to think of church and Christian things as "goody-goody." To help combat this tendency, you might want to ask your pastor or a male church board member to speak to the group about his own "normal" childhood. It may help your guys to discover that the pastor once borrowed a car to go joyriding, dated a lot of girls in college, used to work as a bookie, or whatever. It will also give the speaker an opportunity to explain how he went from being a "normal" guy to a leader of the church. Try to help kids see that much rebellion is destructive, yet there comes a time to rebel against a harmful, sinful lifestyle and dare to find something better.

Step 2

Have group members compete in a "hymn sword drill." Give each participant a hymnal. Explain that you will call out a hymn and a verse number. The first person to stand and read the first line of the verse you asked for wins the round. Play as many rounds as you have time for. Afterward, lead in to a discussion of the things your kids dislike about your church's worship service.

Step 5

Even if your group members don't have an opportunity (or the inclination) to lead a worship service and invigorate it with new and different ideas, they can still make church a more fun place to be. Have them think of an area of the church that they could decorate. Then get permission for them to do so. For example, they might paint a Sunday school room a brighter color. They might make posters or hang streamers. Or they might plan to bring snacks for the entire church one week. While the fun of this exercise seems to be directed toward other people, your group members should discover the sheer joy of working together in a spirit of servanthood. Few will be disappointed with the experience.

Step 1

Perhaps your church's worship service seems too slow-paced for members of the MTV generation. So have your group members imagine that they're the people who put together MTV shows. They should think in terms of how to make the elements of worship more relevant and interesting for young people. What would be the setting? How many people would be involved in each worship service? How could they keep things from dragging? How will they ensure that the focus remains on worshiping Jesus and not merely on being entertained? Have kids struggle with all of these issues. Also challenge them to use as many different media as they can without hindering the flow of the events. When they finish, you might even want to carry out their ideas—if not for the entire congregation, at least among yourselves. While not every worship service needs to be (or ought to be) fast-paced, an occasional "peppy" one would probably be appreciated by everyone.

Step 5

It might help your group members' efforts to act as a consultant group in your church if you videotape the worship service. If this is not done on a regular basis, have someone set up a video camera in an unobtrusive spot to capture the worship service on tape. Later, as group members comment on the things they noted on Repro Resource 6, you'll have the opportunity to locate their specific observations on the videotape and discuss them as a group. Another advantage of a videotape record is that it provides the chance to see exactly how much content of the worship service was overlooked the first time. Kids will probably find significant pieces of information or procedure they missed the first time.

Step 2

Combine Steps 1 and 2 with the following activity. Have kids form groups. Instruct each group to plan an "ideal" Sunday worship service. In planning this service, group members should take into account as many factors as possible. For instance, what time would the service begin? How long would it last? What kinds of hymns or choruses would the congregation sing? Who would perform the special music? What topics would be covered in the pastor's sermon? How long would the sermon last? After a few minutes, have each group share and explain its ideal service. Then lead in to a discussion on what changes *Jesus* might make in your church's worship service.

Step 5

Rather than handing out copies of Repro Resource 6 and trying to tailor the sheet to fit your church, ask kids to "rate" various areas of your church and its worship service. You might have them rate each area on a scale of one to ten (with ten being the highest) by holding up the appropriate number of fingers to indicate their rating. Go through the list on Repro Resource 6, pausing after each category to allow a couple of group members to explain their rating. Then as you wrap up the session, challenge kids to focus on their *personal* worship habits.

Step 2

If you find that your kids are reluctant or unable to identify specific weaknesses in their church, try offering them a biblical "measuring stick." Distribute paper and pencils. As a group, read Psalms 122, 133, and 150. After each psalm is read, have kids grade their church on a scale of one to ten (with ten being the highest) as to how well it practices the principles of that psalm. Group members should come up with three number grades (one for each psalm). When they've done that, they should add up the three numbers to get a "final grade" for the church. Use the following scale as a discussion starter regarding your kids' scores:

- 26-30—The church is riding high!
- 21-25—The church is cruising along nicely.
- 16-20—The church's engine is starting to sputter.
- 11-15—The church is just coasting.
- 0-10—The church's engine is dead!

Step 5

As you wrap up the session, focus on the church's responsibility to its surrounding community. Ask: **On a scale of one to ten—with ten being the highest—how much involvement do the churches in your area have in your community? Explain. How much involvement *should* churches have in their communities? Why? What would you like to see *your* church do for the people in your community?** You might want to use these questions in conjunction with the "church consultant" activity.

Step 4

After you discuss the importance of personal worship, hand out graph paper and pencils. Ask group members to create "spiritual growth graphs." At intervals across the bottom of the page, on a horizontal line, they should write their ages, beginning with age six or so and continuing to their present age. The vertical portion of the graph will indicate degrees of spiritual commitment, with the age line as zero and the top of the page as a maximum level. Ask group members to think back as far as they can remember and create a graph to show periods of spiritual growth, times when they drifted away from God, and so forth. Assure them that most people will have a number of peaks and valleys. Theoretically, we should grow regularly throughout our lives, but most of us face spurts of growth—frequently after a very low period. Obviously your high schoolers will have a few more years to work with than the junior highers. Use this opportunity to see if they are getting closer to God during that time or farther away from Him. Point out that high school usually forces young people to go one direction or the other. Challenge your kids to continue to seek God's wisdom and power no matter what they face.

Step 5

If personal devotions are to become a priority for your group members, many of your kids may need to be accountable to someone. You aren't likely to have enough time to monitor the daily devotions of all group members, so let them hold *each other* accountable. Pair kids together for regular devotions. Challenge them to maintain their personal devotionals every day (or almost every day), but also to get together with their assigned partner at least once a week. Try to team less mature people with those who can help them out (perhaps pairing high schoolers with junior highers). Check in a week or so to see how things are working out.

Step 1

Replace the opening activity with an informal quiz. It's sometimes difficult to tell how much sixth graders know about certain basic spiritual truths, so try to get a feel for your group members' level of understanding before you try to lead this session. You might ask them to define terms such as *prayer, church, body of Christ, fellowship,* etc. Or you might have them try to draw such things using Pictionary rules. Whatever you think your group members would enjoy, watch and listen to see how complete their definitions and perceptions are about such things. If your kids don't have a good grasp of the basics, try to spend some time during the session explaining the concepts more thoroughly. If group members already have a good working knowledge of these spiritual concepts, you can move ahead with the session and build on what they know.

Step 5

When you instruct group members to act as church consultants, be aware that many of your sixth graders may sit with their parents in church. Encourage them to sit together as a group as they take on the responsibility of evaluating the church service. It will help for them to compare observations, point out things to each other that might otherwise be missed, and begin to interact with each other on a positive level rather than simply talking or goofing off during the worship service. Sitting together should also begin to help them feel more "adult"—more like members of an important group instead of mere kids.

Date Used:

Approx. Time

Step 1: Praying Attention _____
o Extra Action
o Mostly Girls
o Media
o Sixth Grade

Step 2: The Problem with Church _____
o Extra Action
o Small Group
o Heard It All Before
o Fellowship & Worship
o Mostly Guys
o Extra Fun
o Short Meeting Time
o Urban

Step 3: Rebel with a Cause _____
o Heard It All Before
o Little Bible Background
o Mostly Guys

Step 4: It's a Secret _____
o Large Group
o Little Bible Background
o Fellowship & Worship
o Mostly Girls
o Combined Jr. High/High School

Step 5: Consultant Results _____
o Small Group
o Large Group
o Extra Fun
o Media
o Short Meeting Time
o Urban
o Combined Jr. High/High School
o Sixth Grade

4 What Would Jesus Do ... with a Family Like Mine?

YOUR GOALS FOR THIS SESSION:

Choose one or more

☐ To help kids see that the problems they face in their families are probably shared by many other group members as well.

☐ To help kids understand that peace in the family is as much up to them as it is to their parents and siblings.

☐ To help kids create a specific plan to minimize problems and become happier within their families.

☐ Other _____
_____

Your Bible Base:

Matthew 13:53-58
John 7:1-13; 19:25-27

The World's Best Family Member

(Needed: Copies of Repro Resource 7, pencils, tray of assorted items, prizes [optional])

Before kids arrive, place a tray of assorted items in the center of the meeting room. These can be any kind of items—just clean out the nearest closet, lost-and-found box, or odds-and-ends drawer. As kids arrive, ask them to familiarize themselves with the items. Then, as you begin the session, have each person select an item that represents his or her family in some way. Ask the person to explain his or her choice to the rest of the group. (For example, "My family is like this old Rubik's Cube, because once it gets out of whack it's almost impossible to get it together again." Or "The members of my family are like this pair of sunglasses because we are rarely completely open with each other. We seem to hide what we really feel.")

Explain: **Most families have problems—especially those that have junior high kids in them. But with a little effort from everyone involved, those problems can be worked out and differences can be settled.**

Of course, some kids are better than others, so we're going to have a "Best Family Member" contest. The first part of the contest will consist of an evaluation. Hand out copies of "The Best-Family-Member-in-the-World Contest" (Repro Resource 7) and pencils. **In the second part of the contest, the top-scoring people will undergo an interview process.**

Once group members complete the sheet, have them score their evaluations by adding together all of their points. (The maximum score is 200.) Call the three people who rated themselves highest to the front of the room. These will be your finalists. Let other group members ask them questions that will determine if they are truly the model children they have determined themselves to be. Group members should be allowed to challenge the answers of the finalists if they know differently. Or they might choose to ask how the finalists would react to certain situations. (For example, "Suppose your parents left you alone with specific instructions to wait for a very important phone call and a warning not to leave the house for any reason. If you then happened to see a hundred-dollar bill blowing across your yard, would you go out to get it?")

After sufficiently quizzing your finalists, let group members vote for who should win by using the old "volume of applause" method. If you wish, award your winner a prize for being your group's "Best Family Member" (or perhaps for being the "Group Member with the Answers Most Like the Ones the Leader Wanted to Hear").

STEP

2

God's Gift to Siblings

Have kids form two groups. Ask each group to put together a skit. Explain that you want both groups to consider what it must have been like for Jesus to have been a "typical" junior higher. Their skits should speculate on what life at home might have been like for Jesus as a young teen. You might preface the skits with this quote from *Halley's Bible Handbook*: "Of [Jesus'] childhood the Bible says little. . . . Jesus was the eldest of a family of [at least] seven children. . . . How we wish we had a glimpse of his home life—how the Son of God as a growing boy bore himself under the daily round of irritations usual in such a situation."

The first group should perform a skit to show Jesus at home, being "bossed around" by His parents. (Group members may want to drop in some of their favorite "hated" phrases that parents seem to use so often.) Knowing that it is God's will for children to obey and honor their parents, how would He have responded to being bossed around? (One possible result of this skit is to show that parents aren't sadistic. If a child does all he or she is asked to do, parents will usually be very pleased and accommodating.)

The second group should place the young Jesus in a more contemporary setting. Have the group members suppose that their parents have agreed to sponsor a transfer student from Israel. The student turns out to be the young Jesus. How would your group members relate to living in the same home with Him? What situations might cause some potential conflict or stress?

As the groups perform their skits, make a list of questions that are raised as to what behaviors Jesus might or might not display. As soon as the skits are over, divide the room into four quarters, designated as (1) Yes, definitely; (2) Probably; (3) Probably not; and (4) Definitely not. Read the questions one at a time. Group members should respond by standing in the appropriate quadrant of the room.

As necessary, use the following questions to supplement the ones you come up with.

OPTIONS

HEARD IT ALL BEFORE

LITTLE BIBLE BACKGROUND

FELLOWSHIP & WORSHIP

MOSTLY GIRLS

MOSTLY GUYS

JR. HIGH HIGH SCHOOL COMBINED

• **Would Jesus ever question a command His parents gave Him?**

• **Would Jesus kiss His parents good-night?**

• **Would Jesus tell on His brothers and sisters when they misbehaved?**

• **Would Jesus ever yell at His brothers and sisters?**

• **Would Jesus ever have to be asked more than once to do something He said He would do?**

• **Would Jesus ever run away from home?**

• **Would Jesus try to grow up to be what His parents wanted Him to be—a doctor, a lawyer, etc.?**

• **Would Jesus ever tell anyone to hate his or her parents?**

This last query is a trick question. In fact, Jesus is quoted in Luke 14:26 as saying, "If anyone comes to me and does not hate his father and mother, his wife and children, his brothers and sisters—yes, even his own life—he cannot be my disciple." The next-to-last question should also provoke some thought. Junior highers are in the process of learning to think and reason for themselves, though most are still expected to do what their parents say. But if Jesus had not sought out His heavenly Father's will for His life, He may have lived a long and safe (and unnoticed) life as a carpenter like His earthly stepfather.

Explain: **Certainly we are to *love* and *obey* our parents according to the teachings of Scripture—and of Jesus. Yet at some point we must make our own decisions in life, particularly in regard to issues such as faith, salvation, and spiritual growth. If, as adults, we discover we cannot follow both the wishes of our parents and the commands of God, we may need to make some hard decisions to put the wishes of Jesus before even the wishes of our parents. Jesus is not telling us to *literally* hate our parents and siblings, yet we are not to allow even these people who are closest to us to interfere with our personal dedication to the Gospel.**

If you have completed Session 2 in this book, review the passage in Luke 2 that describes Jesus' extra days in the temple in Jerusalem after His parents had started home. Say: **When Jesus' parents came to get Him, they couldn't understand why their twelve-year-old boy had done what He did. And even though He could have been arrogant or argumentative, Scripture tells us "He went down to Nazareth with them and was obedient to them." When we think—or even are sure—that we know better than our parents, it is usually right to be obedient to them anyway. When we're older we can determine whether or not to do something other than what they advise.** You may want to mention that certainly exceptions should be made if a child is in an abusive or dangerous environment.

Our Brother Who Art Here among Us

(Needed: Bibles, paper, pencils)

Now that you've speculated on what it might be like for Jesus to interact with a human family, explain that we *are* able to know a little bit about what it was like for Him as a young adult.

Say: **God instituted the family structure, yet it sometimes falls far short of His intentions. Even Jesus' family had its problems. In fact, His family members had the extra burden of trying to cope with a "celebrity" who was followed by crowds, hated by religious leaders, and capable of wondrous and amazing miracles. How do you think Jesus' brothers and sisters felt when He began His public ministry and became so popular? Were they jealous? Doubtful? Confused? Angry?**

Have kids form three groups. Distribute paper and pencils to each group. Assign the following passages for the groups to read and report on:

Group #1—John 7:1-13
Group #2—John 19:25-27
Group #3—Matthew 13:53-58

In addition to explaining the facts of the story, each group should make a list of "principles for understanding and/or improving your family," based on the passage. You might want to suggest that it stands to reason that if Jesus Himself had family problems, we should expect them as well.

Group #1 (John 7:1-13) should see that Jesus' brothers had a problem with sibling rivalry. They seemed to be trying to get rid of Him. Even though they didn't believe in Him, they were trying to convince Him to "go public." Perhaps they thought if He became a famous person they wouldn't have to deal with Him anymore. Maybe they thought He would only embarrass Himself. Or were they aware that the Jewish leaders wanted to take His life? Whatever their motives, Jesus had to live with the problems that resulted.

Here are a few family principles that might come from this passage:

• Being good is not an absolute guarantee for getting along with family members. Families contain a number of imperfect people. No matter how pure one person is, problems can arise from others.

• Be yourself, not who someone else wants you to be.

• Evaluate the advice you receive from other family members.

• Find a way to put up with the problems you face. (For Jesus it meant sending His brothers off on their own while He kept to Himself.)

Group #2 (John 19:25-27) will discover that even when Jesus was dying on the cross, He was concerned about His mother's well-being. (It is generally assumed that His stepfather, Joseph, was no longer living at this time.) Even though Jesus had gotten in trouble with the law, had been accused of terrible things by the religious leaders, and was hanging on a cross as a public spectacle of humiliation, He wanted to do what He could for His mother.

Here are a few family principles that might come from this passage:

• No matter how old you get, don't lose your basic commitment to your parents. (Therefore, we should do what we can not to weaken or sever the relationship during our junior high or high school years.)

• When a parent-child relationship is good, you can expect that no matter how grim your circumstances get, your parents will be there for you. (And if the situation is reversed, you will be there for them.)

• Even though parents may not understand or agree with everything you do, they may still love you unconditionally.

Group #3 (Matthew 13:53-58) will deal more with the issue of family reputation. After becoming a public figure and amazing people throughout the area with His teachings, Jesus returned to His hometown. But when He got there, the townspeople couldn't appreciate Him for who He had become. They recited the names of His other family members as if to suggest, "Since the rest of His family are 'nobodies,' what makes Him think He's so special?" The family's reputation can have an effect on its individuals.

Here are a few family principles that might come from this passage:

• Sometimes we have to rise above, or perhaps struggle to live up to, the reputations of our families.

• People who put down you or your family a lot aren't necessarily right.

• People may judge our families as a group, but God will reward us as individuals. (So we can be supportive of our families, yet shouldn't let them hold us back if we sense that God has bigger plans for us than they do.)

These suggested principles are simply starting points. Your group members may come up with answers that are completely different, but even more meaningful to them.

STEP 4

The Good, the Bad, and the Family

Of course, the whole reason we need to create principles to understand and get along better in our families is that families aren't perfect. Yet each person may tend to feel that the problems in his or her family are abnormal. The assumption may be that other families are like the Cleavers while one's own nuclear unit is more like the Addams Family. So spend a few minutes having everyone share his or her concerns and complaints by completing this sentence: "The worst thing about my family is . . ." Be sure group members think in terms of brothers and sisters (and even extended family) as well as parents. They may discover they share more complaints than they would have expected and will begin to empathize more with each other.

Then, when everyone has had a say, explain that it's easy to focus on what is wrong with families. So go around again and have each person complete this sentence: "The *best* thing about my family is . . ."

Help kids see that all families have their good *and* bad points. No family is perfect, nor is any family likely to be so completely terrible that it's worth giving up on. Explain that no matter what problems someone may be facing in his or her family, he or she can usually do *something* to begin to remedy the problem—even if no one else in the family seems willing to do so.

STEP 5

Today's Special: Complaints

(Needed: Cut-apart copies of Repro Resource 8, chalkboard and chalk or newsprint and marker)

Point out that when we face problems in our families, there are many options we can choose. The tendency may be to wait for parents to take action, but in many cases young people can play an active role in resolving family conflict. So have group members think of the "worst

O P T I O N S

things" they listed in Step 4 and then brainstorm ways that *they* might be able to make those situations better.

After compiling a list on the board, point out that even when your group members can't take an active role in making a bad situation better, they can take a *passive* one. On your list on the board you might want to include such options as being patient, not talking back even when parents might be wrong (and waiting for a better time to discuss the problem), and so forth. Explain that many times the things we *don't* do will improve a situation more than the things we actually try to do.

With this in mind, point out that the one thing that almost *never* works is complaining. Yet many times that is the most common course of action for young people. Summarize: **It's natural to complain when we don't like something or when we feel we're being treated unfairly. Yet if we don't set some limits on how much we complain, we tend to do it all of the time. Then our parents and other family members stop listening to what we have to say, even when we are trying to be helpful.**

Hand out "Complaint Coupons" (Repro Resource 8). (These should have been copied and cut apart prior to the session.) Explain that each time group members complain to a parent or family member this week, they should give up one of their coupons. Most parents understand that a certain amount of complaining is to be expected. But when the coupons run out, group members are no longer entitled to complain. Also explain that simply because they complain about something doesn't mean that the parent or family member must do what the young person wants. The coupon simply entitles him or her to strongly disagree. Determine as a group how many coupons each person should receive for the week. Also send home the parental explanation sheet that is included on Repro Resource 8 so the parents will understand how this activity should work. Then, at your next meeting, see if anyone has any coupons left (and how many people used theirs up on the first day).

Point out that you're not attempting to have group members deny what they are feeling. Emotions are natural and healthy. Yet there are usually constructive steps to take within our families when things don't go our way. Complaining is too negative and too easy. We need to work a bit harder to have the kind of families that pull together during hard times and are there for us when we need them.

Close with a prayer, specifically to give thanks for the families of your group members and to ask for the wisdom and perseverance to live at peace with family members as much of the time as possible.

EXTRA ACTION

Step 1

Rather than using existing objects to represent families in some way or another, hand out modeling clay and let group members create their own objects, shapes, or whatever. For example, you could start by having them create something to symbolize their families. Then they could form something to represent their *usual* feelings toward their families, their *current* attitude toward family members, the thing that holds their family together, something that interferes with family togetherness, and so forth. Most young people are good at creating symbols to represent feelings, attitudes, and other intangible concepts, so don't be reluctant to let them try.

Step 4

Rather than merely having group members name the best and worst things about their families, use charades to do the same thing. One at a time, let group members act out what they consider to be the worst thing about their families. Then have them act out what they consider to be the best thing about their families. Keep the activity moving quickly, or it can drag out. If you keep up the pace, it probably won't take long for others to guess what each person is acting out.

SMALL GROUP

Step 3

Rather than having kids form small groups to cover all three passages, focus solely on John 7:1-13. Work on it as a group and then discuss it thoroughly, searching for practical application as you do. Ask: **Do you think Jesus fit in with His family? Why or why not? Do you ever feel left out of something the rest of your family likes to do? What can you learn from Jesus to help you deal with conflict or differences of opinion within the family? What else can you learn about family matters from this passage?** With a small group, make the most of the opportunity to interact with one another and offer support.

Step 5

As part of the application of the material in this session, challenge kids to see fellow group members as a "family" of sorts. Ask: **How are we like a family? What are some things we can do to grow closer together? In what ways might this group be even better than your flesh-and-blood family?** In many cases, young people are able to be more open about problems and concerns with their peers in a safe environment rather than at home where they may feel they're being "grilled" by their parents. Try to do whatever you can to develop the feeling of family, perhaps even to the point of planning some meals together, sharing responsibilities and advice, and so forth.

LARGE GROUP

Step 1

Begin the meeting in an extremely small and cramped area. You may want to remove all chairs and have group members sit on the floor, with no room to stretch or get comfortable. See how far you can get in the session before kids start to complain or get on one another's nerves. At that point, move to a larger and more comfortable area to discuss how sometimes family problems can result from similar conditions of "not enough space" within the confines of one's house. Suggest that when we sense others are "cramping our style," we can choose to retreat and carve out some space for ourselves, rather than making life needlessly miserable for everyone else.

Step 3

One advantage of a large group is being able to capitalize on the numerous insights and opinions on any given topic or passage. So when you get ready to do the Bible study, don't limit the number of groups to three. Form as many small groups as you can. Have several of them study each of the three passages given in the session. Ask the members of each small group to look closely for *three* principles for getting along better with their families. After a few minutes, have each group share its list of principles. While you're almost certain to get a bit of duplication, it may be surprising to see how varied some of the principles are from groups who studied the same passage. What may seem very clear to one group may have been missed completely by another.

Step 2

After reminding group members of Jesus' attitude when His parents found Him in the temple, point out that they can (and should) imitate His example. To help them remember this, have them create a slogan based on the story and then make buttons or posters to broadcast the slogan. For example, they might come up with "Don't Push It!" as a catchy reminder that even though they may be right in disagreeing with a friend or family member, they can choose to be submissive as well. After several group members have offered ideas for slogans, choose one as a group to use for your buttons or posters. Encourage group members to remind one another of the slogan during stressful times when someone may seem to have forgotten about it.

Step 5

Distribute paper and pencils. Instruct group members to write a description of a typical day in their family. In their descriptions, they should include information about what time each family member gets up; what it's like trying to get ready in the morning; which family members go to work, which ones go to school, and which ones stay home; what time everyone gets home; what everyone does in the evening; what time each person goes to bed; etc. After a few minutes, collect the sheets and shuffle them. Then read each one aloud while group members try to guess whose it is. Afterward, emphasize that for better or worse, all families are unique.

Step 1

If your group members don't know a lot about the Bible, perhaps their parents don't either. If this is true, you might want to plan a "parents night" to present the material in this session. The parents might benefit just as much as the kids from a session on family relationships. In addition, this can be a natural opportunity to help both kids and their parents get a bit more comfortable with a church setting. You have something specific to offer since the teaching is more practical than theological. Almost every parent has the desire to do a good job raising kids. If you can provide good suggestions and challenge kids and parents simultaneously, who knows what might happen in the lives of your group members?

Step 2

Kids don't need a lot of Bible background to know what it's like to experience sibling rivalry. Start with your group members' feelings about their brothers and sisters as you work your way into the Bible study. In addition to the agree/disagree questions about Jesus in the session, use the following discussion questions: **What would it feel like to have a brother who was a lot more popular than you? If you were jealous, what are some things you might do to "get even"? What would it be like to realize that your brother could "zap" you if he wanted to? Would you be more likely to ignore him, or to see how much you could get by with?** The Bible passages don't say much about Jesus and His siblings. The more you can help your group members learn to "read between the lines," the better they should be able to remember and apply the Bible to their own lives.

Step 2

Have someone read Matthew 12:46-50. Point out that Jesus didn't limit His definition of "family" to those who were related to Him by flesh and blood. Rather, He included "whoever does the will of my Father in heaven." Using this definition, ask group members to expand *their* "families" this week. Have each person think of at least three people with whom he or she could spend time during the next week in an attempt to develop a sense of family. Point out that so far in life, your junior highers have had little inclination or opportunity to go beyond the concept of the nuclear family. But someday many of them will be going to college, jobs in other areas, or perhaps military service. When they do, they need to know how to make new friends and create an "extended family."

Step 5

Close the session by putting together an impromptu worship time based on the family aspect of Christian faith—one that acknowledges what it means to be a member of the "family of God." Ask group members to tell you everything they know about being part of this family. They may wish to draw from Bible verses, songs, choruses, etc. (Romans 8:15-17 is an excellent passage that deals with spiritual adoption, the privilege of calling God "Father," the rights of being co-heirs with Christ, and much more.) Remind group members that when they face problems in their *human* families, they should always remember that they can find unconditional love, forgiveness, and acceptance as a valued member of the family of God.

MOSTLY GIRLS

Step 2
Use the following questions to supplement your discussion of Jesus: **Does the fact that Jesus was a man make it more difficult for you to identify with Him? Why or why not? If you were Jesus' sister, what do you think you would most admire about Him? Why? Do you think it would be difficult to grow up with a brother who never did anything wrong? Explain.**

Step 5
In addition to using their "Complaint Coupons" this week, you may also wish to have your girls keep track of the things they complain about throughout the week. Then they can look at the list to see if there's a pattern or theme to their complaints. This may help your girls identify a specific trouble spot that needs some healing and/or discussion. Make yourself available to help group members with any problems they may wish to discuss.

MOSTLY GUYS

Step 1
The opening activity in the session may be a bit too abstract for some guys (who usually prefer a more direct approach). Instead, simply have group members complete the following sentences:
• **My family is so weird that . . .**
• **There's nothing wrong with my family that a good _____ wouldn't fix!**
• **If I turn out to be just like my parents, I think I'll . . .**
• **I think I could do without my family, except when . . .**
    Some of the answers you receive may be exaggerated or comedic, but that's OK. Most will have a root of truth that will introduce problems or matters of concern to your guys. So as you go through the session, you'll be better prepared to deal with specifics rather than abstract concepts.

Step 2
As you talk about how Jesus would likely respond in a number of home situations, try to emphasize to your guys that real men don't always need to prove that they're more correct, stronger, or more aggressive than everyone else. Sometimes they need to prove (like Jesus did) that they can take whatever anyone else can dish out, and then walk away—especially in family conflicts in which they have little to gain by pressing a point. You might even want to plan a "Nothing Fazes Me Night" for your guys. They should agree for a specified amount of time to live at peace with all family members—to neither provoke an argument nor respond in a way that would allow someone else to start one. This may sound easy, but is likely to be more difficult than kids think. (You may also want to mention this night to some of the parents, so they can monitor group members' success.)

EXTRA FUN

Step 1
A fun thing to do while you have a tray full of items on hand is play a memory game. Make sure you have at least twenty items on the tray. Keep the tray covered until you give a signal. Then, after letting the kids study the items for thirty seconds or so, cover the tray again. Hand out paper and pencils. Then have group members list all of the things they remember seeing on the tray. See which of your group members have the best memories. Later in the session, you can refer to how often we have "short-term memory" when it comes to how we act toward other family members. We know how we're *supposed* to treat them, but frequently we just don't take the time to recall what we know and put it into practice.

Step 3
Begin this step with some role-reversal skits. Sometimes during conflicts with parents, kids get so accustomed to using their same old arguments that they hardly know what they're saying. So have some fun by letting group members play the roles of their parents while adults play the roles of kids. (If necessary, recruit some adults from the church for this activity.) Create some scenes in which your "kids" are trying to convince their "parents" to let them buy an expensive jacket, host a major party, buy a drum set, etc. Note the responses of the "parents." Do they say no while roleplaying adults simply because that's what they would expect to hear as kids? Or will they come up with several valid considerations before deciding whether to allow their "kids" to act on their wishes? After doing these skits and then discussing the problems Jesus faced in His family, group members may be able to recognize the many factors that are involved in making decisions—both on the part of parents in response to kids' requests, and for young people trying to keep peace within a family.

MEDIA

SHORT MEETING **TIME**

URBAN

Step 1

After everyone has filled out the questionnaire on Repro Resource 7 and the top-scoring people have been announced, create a "media event." Have kids form groups, and let each group "campaign" for one of the "candidates." Instruct the groups to model their efforts after political campaigns as they write slogans, make posters, put together TV "ads," and so forth. After a few minutes, let each group make its presentation. You or some other impartial adult might want to evaluate the groups' campaigns based on effectiveness of the message, creativity, honesty, and so forth.

Step 4

Rather than simply having group members express the best and worst things about their families, set up the room to resemble a talk show (Donahue, Oprah, or one of your favorites). Explain that today's topic is "Weird Families and the Strange Junior Highers Who Belong to Them." Wander around the room, soliciting comments about families. Whenever someone shares a "best" or "worst" thing, turn to the rest of the "audience" to see if they've been through a similar experience. You, as "host," might also take on an aggressive demeanor and challenge group members' answers. ("Oh, come on! Do you expect us to believe that's the worst thing about your family? Tell us how you *really* feel!") If you have access to a video camera, have someone tape the "show" so you can refer back to group members' comments if you need to.

Step 1

If you want to cover a lot of material quickly, one option is to conduct your own "Family Feud" survey prior to the session. Talk to a number of parents and get their opinions on questions such as the following:

• **What is the major source of conflict in families?**
• **What is your favorite family tradition?**
• **What word or phrase do parents use perhaps a bit too often in your home?**
• **What word or phrase do kids use perhaps a bit too often in your home?**
• **How many times each hour would you say the average teenager complains about something?**
• **What is the least effective form of discipline/punishment used in your home?**

After getting answers from a number of parents, compute percentages to use for points. Then, to begin the session, play the game with your group members according to "Family Feud" rules. After playing the game, make appropriate comments about each problem area discussed.

Step 4

If you're really short on time, combine Steps 3 and 4. Instead of having kids form small groups to report on the Scripture passages, go through the passages as a group. (Be sure to emphasize the principles outlined in the session.) During the Bible study, pass around two sheets of paper. At the top of one sheet, write "The worst thing about my family is . . ."; at the top of the other sheet, write "The best thing about my family is . . ." Have group members complete these statements and then pass the sheets on. At the end of the Bible study, collect the sheets and read aloud some of your group members' comments.

Step 1

For a more accurate reading of your group members' family lives, have kids go through Repro Resource 7 again—this time marking an "X" on the scores that they believe their *family members* would give them. It's likely that at least some of these scores will be lower than the ones group members gave themselves. When kids have finished marking the second set of answers, have them add up the scores. Then have them compare the total from their second set of answers with the total from the first set. How much lower is the second total? As a group, discuss why family members might view us differently than we view ourselves.

Step 4

Try using a brief object lesson to illustrate the point that good and bad things can be found in almost any family. Pass around an overripe apple—one that has gone bad in many spots, but is still edible. Say: **This apple is like most people's family life: There are good and rotten areas. But with God's help, the rotten can be sliced away while the good remains.** Using a knife, cut away the rotten parts of the apple, leaving only that which is edible. Then eat the remaining part of the apple.

Step 2

Before the session, ask a junior higher to imagine that he or she is Jesus during the next few minutes. He or she should make mental notes of things that happen during the opening exercises that might capture Jesus' attention. The person shouldn't act any differently toward others, but should simply look for exemplary actions or areas that need improvement. When you get to Step 2 and begin to discuss how Jesus might respond in certain situations, let your volunteer report on what he or she has witnessed. Explain that even though the topic of the session is family relationships, the applications are the same. If older or stronger people tend to dominate others in a group setting, they're likely to do the same thing at home.

Step 5

When kids disagree with parental rules, there are several options they can pursue: obey, throw a tantrum, rebel, complain, etc. Another option you might want to consider as a group is negotiation. Since young people are getting older and more capable of making their own decisions, they need to learn to reason with authority figures with whom they disagree. Set up some roleplays in which junior highers play themselves and high schoolers play their parents. The situations should involve the "parents" taking a very strict stand and the "children" wanting more freedom. Have the kids practice negotiating. See if they reach a point where they can agree that if the child meets certain criteria, the parents will allow a particular privilege. If the negotiations go well between your high schoolers and junior highers, you might suggest that kids find appropriate opportunities to try negotiating at home.

Step 4

Older kids are likely to be able to think of the worst things about their families and automatically begin to think of ways to work them out. Once they identify the problem, the solutions are sometimes fairly simple. But younger kids may need some help realizing that they might be able to take the initiative to alleviate a problem. So after each person names the worst thing about his or her family, have the rest of the group members brainstorm ideas to help the person improve the situation. Some kids may be able to share out of personal experience. Others can offer fresh ideas and impartial insight. Young people may resist the advice of parents, teachers, or other authority figures. But if the same advice comes from a peer, they may be much more willing to try it.

Step 5

Have all of your group members take hold (using only one hand) of a dollar bill at the same time. Explain that the person who holds on longest can keep it. See what happens in the tug-of-war that ensues. It may be that the dollar bill is ripped apart. Or perhaps one person will get it at the expense of all the others. Explain that families can be similarly damaged if we decide to do what *we* want to do—no matter what. Sixth graders are probably still very close to their parents. Now is a good time to challenge them to remain that way. Encourage them to be pliable as they go through adolescence—to yield to their parents' wishes much of the time even as they are developing their own unique personalities. If they aren't willing to give in a little bit, the family is likely to tear apart.

Planning Checklist

Date Used:

Approx. Time

Step 1: The World's Best Family Member _____
o Extra Action
o Large Group
o Little Bible Background
o Mostly Guys
o Extra Fun
o Media
o Short Meeting Time
o Urban

Step 2: God's Gift to Siblings _____
o Heard It All Before
o Little Bible Background
o Fellowship & Worship
o Mostly Girls
o Mostly Guys
o Combined Jr. High/High School

Step 3: Our Brother Who Art Here among Us _____
o Small Group
o Large Group
o Extra Fun

Step 4: The Good, the Bad, and the Family _____
o Extra Action
o Media
o Short Meeting Time
o Urban
o Sixth Grade

Step 5: Today's Special: Complaints _____
o Small Group
o Heard It All Before
o Fellowship & Worship
o Mostly Girls
o Combined Jr. High/High School
o Sixth Grade

What Would Jesus Do ... with Friends Like Mine?

YOUR GOALS FOR THIS SESSION:

Choose one or more

☐ To help kids see that friendships can be established with various levels of commitment, and to challenge them to pursue positive and productive relationships.

☐ To help kids understand that they can relate to Jesus as a friend.

☐ To have kids discover more about others in the group and find common bonds that will help them strengthen current friendships and begin new ones.

☐ Other _____
_____

Your Bible Base:

Proverbs 27:17
Matthew 14:22-33;
    16:13-28; 26:69-75
Luke 5:1-11
John 15:12-17; 21:15-19

Friendship Criteria

(Needed: Copies of Repro Resource 9, pencils)

Hand out copies of "Acme Build-Your-Own-Friend Design Kit" (Repro Resource 9) and pencils as kids arrive. Instruct group members to design the "perfect" friend. When they finish, have some volunteers describe the friends they created.

Then ask: **How similar is your description to a good friend you *already* have?** It may be common for young people to describe someone they know rather than conceptualize new possibilities. Have them consider that they have already put a lot of time and energy into existing relationships, and have learned to see the best in each other while overlooking most shortcomings. These friendships may seem "perfect" only because the friends have learned to like each other "as is." Rather than *perfect,* the relationship may be better described as comfortable and familiar.

How similar is your description to yourself? A person who lists his or her own qualities as those desired from a "perfect" friend might tend to feel that those are qualities *anyone* would look for. However, such people may have trouble making friends with people who have a different set of behaviors and characteristics.

If we are aware of what people are looking for in a friend, why aren't we better friends to more people? (It's one thing to *know* that people want unconditional love, forgiveness, and such qualities; it's quite another to *demonstrate* such characteristics consistently.)

Would you say that your "perfect" friend is stronger or weaker than you are? In what ways? Sometimes young people choose friends who aren't as strong or pretty as they are so they don't feel threatened. Others tend to gravitate toward more dynamic personalities who can provide them with a lot of friends, adventure, or other benefits. Both of these extremes can be based on selfish concerns and may need to be avoided.

Dream Come True?

Have a group of volunteers perform a skit. One person (perhaps a small person, but one who can take a lot of verbal chiding) should be the Victim. A number of others should be Tormentors who subject the Victim to a lot of merciless teasing, name-calling, and so forth. Ask the Tormentors to, as much as possible, use names and insults that they actually hear at school or in their neighborhoods. The Victim can try to defend himself verbally, though the others should outnumber him in size, number, and volume—making his attempts to endure the experience rather feeble.

After a while, stop the skit and "run it ahead" to the next day. Explain: **The group of tormentors tells the victim to return tomorrow, or they'll hunt him down and do even worse things to him. Their last words are "Don't make us come looking for you, or you'll be doubly sorry!" That night the victim doesn't sleep well, but at one point he dreams that he has the incredible power to do anything he wants to anyone. When he awakes, he finds that he actually has this power! When the neighbor's yipping chihuahua won't shut up, he says, "I wish that dog's lips were glued together for ten minutes so I could get some peace and quiet." Instantly the sound changes from a high-pitched bark to a rather confused whine. A few other experiments confirm that he can do *anything* he wants: grow an extra nose—temporarily—on his sister's forehead, shrink cattle to the size of Barbie dolls, or whatever. Now, armed with his new ability, it's time for him to meet his tormentors again.**

Resume the skit as the Victim approaches the group of Tormentors. But this time, the Victim can stop the action at any point and use his power if he so desires. He can simply say "Freeze," have the action come to a stop, and then explain what he wants done to each person.

Watch closely. Will the victim retaliate against his aggressors? If so, does he inflict the entire group at once or "pick them off" one at a time? Does he go after the leader only and see if the others then back off? After giving the Victim time to act, thank the skit participants and have them rejoin the group.

Ask: **What things would others of you have done to someone who treated you this way?**

OPTIONS

HEARD IT ALL BEFORE

MOSTLY GIRLS

MOSTLY GUYS

URBAN

Do you think the victim was (or **would have been**) **justified in using his power? Why?**

What *positive* **changes would you like to make in your enemies—or even your friends—that would make them more fun to be around?**

Explain that when Jesus was on earth, His situation wasn't much different from that of the victim in your skit. He was called names, made fun of, and criticized in numerous ways. He also had miraculous power at His disposal. But Jesus never used His power to harm anyone, or even (ordinarily) to get Himself out of a jam. It was used to help others. Rather than dwell on the torments and chiding of His enemies, Jesus focused on the positive things He could do with His friends and those who believed in Him. We can learn a lot from His example.

A Friend in Deed

(Needed: Bibles, paper, pencils, chalkboard and chalk or newsprint and markers)

O P T I O N S

EXTRA ACTION

SMALL GROUP

LARGE GROUP

LITTLE BIBLE BACKGROUND

FELLOWSHIP & WORSHIP

Some of the sessions in this book have been (by necessity) somewhat speculative. We have no written record of how Jesus behaved in school, at home as a young teenager, and so forth. But we *can* see how He treated His friends—at least as an adult. In fact, there is far too much written about Jesus' relationships to cover in one meeting. This section will narrow the focus by examining a few "snapshots" of Jesus' friendship with one person—Peter.

Have kids form four groups. Assign one of the following "snapshots" to each group:

Group #1—Luke 5:1-11
Group #2—Matthew 14:22-33
Group #3—Matthew 16:13-28
Group #4—Matthew 26:69-75; John 21:15-19

Instruct the groups to read and discuss their assigned passages, and to write down anything they think is important for us to learn about friendship from the things Jesus and Peter (Simon) did together. After the groups have covered the material and compiled their lists, discuss their findings. At this point, try to keep the discussion and applications on an interpersonal level. Even though Peter was relating to Jesus (who was God), look for things that apply to a person-to-person relationship rather than making person-to-God applications.

Group #1 will look at one of Peter's first encounters with Jesus. Among other things, the group should discover that

• Jesus chose friends not for what they could do for Him, but for what He could do for them.

• Surprising things can happen when we lend our possessions to friends (as Peter discovered when he let Jesus use his boat).

• The advice of friends is worthwhile even when we feel we may know more than they do about a particular subject. (Even though Peter was an experienced fisherman, he obeyed Jesus' instructions—and benefited by doing so.)

• Some friendships in life will be more important than others, and deserve more of our time and energy. While we certainly shouldn't exclude people who want to be our friends, some of our relationships improve our lives while others don't. We need to devote more energy to relationships that will improve our lives rather than those that tempt us to do wrong or simply waste our time.

• People are more important than possessions. (Peter "left everything" to follow Jesus.)

Group #2 will examine a pastime that Jesus and Peter shared: walking on water. Among other things, the group should discover that

• Even our closest friends need a little "space" to be to themselves (as Jesus did).

• When situations seem strange, close friends encourage us (vs. 27).

• Friends should support each other in taking healthy risks (vss. 28, 29).

• The expectations we have for our close friends may be higher than for other people. (Jesus chided Peter's lack of faith [vs. 31] even though Peter was the only one of the twelve who had ventured out of the boat.)

Group #3 should discuss Peter's confession of faith to Jesus, followed almost immediately by his inability to understand Jesus' mission. Among other things, the group should discover that

• Close friends have insight into each other that others don't. (While Peter's insight in this case was clearly God-given, the principle holds true in other cases as well. Time spent together and shared intimacies allow close friends to better understand each other.)

• Friends trust each other with responsibility (vs. 18).

• Friends trust each other with secrets that other people may not be able to cope with or keep to themselves (vss. 20, 21).

• True friends should be able to deal with the truth about each other—no matter how distressing that truth might be (vss. 22, 23).

• As close as we are to our friends, we should make sure we're even closer to God—for our own good as well as for theirs (vs. 23).

• Friends must make sacrifices in other areas to keep the friendship strong (vss. 24-28).

Group #4 will see Peter's denial of Jesus, followed by Jesus' post-resurrection reconciliation with Peter. Among other things, the group should discover that

• Personal fear can damage or destroy relationships.

• During stressful situations (like Jesus' arrest), even little things can seem threatening. For Peter, all it took was a couple of servant girls. For us, other things seem more dangerous than usual.

• Letting down a friend, for any reason, can be emotionally traumatic for both people (Matthew 26:75).

• True friends will forgive any offense against them (John 21:15-17).

• Close friends can talk about difficult subjects, even death (John 21:18, 19).

As the groups report on their findings, try to compile a master list of "Friendship Principles" on the board (using only a word or two to abbreviate each principle.) Later in the session you will refer back to specific principles.

Friends in High Places

(Needed: Bibles, Repro Resource 9, list of friendship principles from Step 3)

Explain that the passages you examined concerning the relationship between Jesus and Peter provide a rich source from which we can draw principles to develop better friendships of our own. However, someone may point out that Peter had it easy. With Jesus as his friend, Peter could always be forgiven, always feel accepted and challenged, and so forth. Some young people may feel that their friends don't quite measure up to that standard.

Have someone read John 15:12-17. Many times this passage is used because of Jesus' command to "love each other." But this time point out that Jesus makes a significant change in the "status" of people who follow Him. He continues to be their Master, but *He also becomes their friend.*

Ask: **What do you think is the most important benefit of being a friend of Jesus? What do you think is the greatest responsibility?** Get a few responses.

Instruct group members to review their completed copies of Repro Resource 9. Then ask: **What qualities were you looking for in the "perfect" friend? Other than specific physical specifica-**

tions, how well does Jesus meet the descriptions you gave?

Refer again to the list of "Friendship Principles" compiled in Step 3. Ask: **Since Jesus has declared Himself to be our friend, what are some things from this list we can count on Him doing for us?**

What makes Jesus a *unique* friend? What can He do as our friend that no one else can do? It should be obvious that Jesus is the only *perfect* friend. His love is completely unconditional. His forgiveness is complete. His support and encouragement is unmatched. And with Jesus as a *best* friend, all of our other friendships grow stronger as well.

Is there anything you're looking for in a friend that Jesus *can't* provide? If young people are honest, a few may admit to occasionally looking to their friends to be "accomplices" in some activity they shouldn't be involved in. Older kids might want friends to be "drinking buddies." Younger ones may look for friends who will help them cheat on tests, copy homework, shoplift, experiment with smoking, and so forth. Many of these activities are rarely done on an individual level. Young people look for allies so they won't have to "take the rap" alone if they happen to get caught. Point out that Jesus is not that kind of "friend." A true friend will help others rise above such tendencies and do other things that will accomplish the same purposes (study with the person instead of cheating, loaning money instead of stealing, going bungee-jumping in search of adventure rather than smoking, etc.).

Have someone read Proverbs 27:17: "As iron sharpens iron, so one man sharpens another." Challenge your group members to become "sharpening" friends—people who have a positive influence of growth and self-improvement on each other.

Common Bond Bingo

(Needed: Copies of Repro Resource 10, pencils)

Ask: **Are there people you know whom you *shouldn't* be friendly with?** This may be a difficult question for some junior highers. As children, they were taught to avoid strangers. Yet as they near adulthood, your group members need to become a bit less reclusive and more open to new opportunities for relationships. It's easy to get within a group (clique) and not have to worry about people outside that

O P T I O N S

group—especially when other people may have reputations as trouble-makers, dweebs, snobs, or whatever. It's easier to write off such people for their negative characteristics rather than considering that they may have positive ones as well.

Summarize: **One reason so many people liked Jesus as a friend is that He liked them first. A person's reputation— what he or she had done in the past—didn't matter to Jesus. The important thing was what He could do for that person. And one of Jesus' best methods of making new friends was finding common bonds. With Simon Peter and Andrew, He started out by talking about fishing** (Mark 1:16-18). **With religious leaders, He used logic and knowledge to pique their interest** (John 3:1-21). **And with an unknown woman from another area—one whom most other men of His land would have avoided—He got a conversation started with the common bond of being thirsty** (John 4:1-26). **Many times the people who started out as strangers ended up as His friends and disciples.**

Explain that we can make friends with people we don't expect to be our friends if we start by finding something in common with those people. Even within your group there may be undiscovered common bonds that could help bring members closer together. Hand out copies of "Common Bond Bingo" (Repro Resource 10). See who can collect the most initials during the time you have left. And after group members get the hang of things to look for, challenge them to try the same thing with people at school—people who may seem lonely, overlooked, or otherwise in need of a friend. It's what Jesus would have done. And who knows? Just a bit of effort on the part of your group members this week might result in new (and lifelong) friendships.

Acme Build-Your-Own-Friend Design Kit

You want friends, right? You pick and choose from all of the available options, but it seems so difficult to find someone who fits all of your criteria *perfectly*. Well, that's where we come in. We here at Acme Design-a-Friend want to help. Here is one of our sample forms for you to fill out. When you get finished, send us your specs. We'll search our vast files and deliver your new friend to you for a lifetime of friendship pleasure.

GENDER OF NEW FRIEND: o Male   o Female

DESIRED HEIGHT: _____

DESIRED WEIGHT: _____

DESIRED AGE: _____

HAIR COLOR: o Blond   o Black   o Brown   o Red   o Other: _____

HAIR STYLE: o Buzz cut   o Dreadlocks   o Beehive   o Other : _____

EYE COLOR: o Brown   o Blue   o Green   o Red   o Other: _____

APPEARANCE: o Drop-dead gorgeous   o Nice looking   o Pretty plain

OPTIONS:	YES	NO
Glasses	o	o
Contacts	o	o
Dandruff	o	o
Dimples	o	o
Freckles	o	o
Perfect suntan	o	o
"Genius" IQ	o	o

Other requests: _____

INTERESTS:
What extracurricular activities should this person be involved in?

What hobbies should this person enjoy?

SOCIAL LIFE: o Heavy dater   o Occasional dater   o Never dates

POPULARITY: o One of the cool people   o Average   o Kind of a dweeb

OTHER DESIRED "CUSTOMIZED" SPECIFICATIONS (qualities, strengths, weaknesses, etc.):

COMMON BOND BINGO

One of the secrets to making new friends and strengthening existing friendships is to find things you and other people have in common. So look for the following common bonds between you and other people in the group. When you find someone who fits a category, have him or her initial the appropriate square. However, you may use each person for only one category. The purpose is to see how many "bingos" you can get (up, down, or diagonally), so you may want to strategize a bit before letting people fill in the first category that applies.

Someone with a parent who has the same first, middle, or last name as one of your parents	Someone with the same hobby as you	Someone with the same teacher as you	Someone with the same favorite dessert as you	Someone with the same favorite sports team as you
Someone born the same month as you (regardless of age)	Someone the same height as you	Someone with the same number of brothers and sisters as you	Someone with the same favorite soft drink as you	Someone you've recently eaten a meal with
Someone you genuinely admire	Someone who shares your fondness for an unusual food or activity	FREE SPACE	Someone you would be willing to sing a duet with	Someone dressed in the same color as you are
Someone who knows one of your secrets	Someone whose voice sounds a little (or a lot) like yours	Someone with the same hair color as you	Someone just like you in terms of whether or not you wear braces and glasses/contacts	Someone just like you in terms of being right-handed or left-handed
Someone with the same favorite musical group as you	Someone with the same number of living grandparents as you	Someone with the same number of pets as you	Someone who enjoys your favorite board game or video game	Someone with the same hair length (or very close) as you

Step 1

Begin the session with a drawing game (similar to Pictionary). Have kids form teams. Distribute paper and pencils to each team. Then allow one volunteer from each team to see the word he or she is to draw. At your signal, volunteers will begin to draw something to help their teammates guess the word. (Drawers may not use letters or symbols.) The first team to guess correctly wins a point. Play several rounds, using different drawers each time. The words you use for the game should represent characteristics of relationships. Some might be traits of true friendship, such as *honesty, communication, encouragement,* and *sacrifice.* Others might be symptoms of poor friendships, such as *gossip, flattery, put-downs, selfishness, jealousy,* and *conceit.* At the end of the game, have group members think back to what they've drawn and separate the qualities they want in their friendships from those they hope to avoid.

Step 3

As each group discusses its assigned passage, have the members try to think of a similar incident in their own lives. They should then prepare a skit based on that incident. For instance, Group #1 might come up with a skit in which someone leaves one kind of lifestyle as soon as he or she makes a new friend who shows him or her a better way to live. Group #2 might come up with a skit about friends who challenge each other to greater levels of adventure and faith. Group #3 might come up with a skit about friends who see the best in each other. Group #4 might come up with a skit in which someone is forgiven for a terrible offense by a good friend. If groups need assistance, give general suggestions, but leave it up to them to come up with specifics. After each group presents its skit, the members should explain what it had to do with the Bible story they read.

Step 3

Rather than using all four passages, focus solely on Luke 5:1-11. After reading the passage as a group, direct the discussion to the selection of Jesus' other disciples. Ask: **Why do you think Jesus limited the number of His disciples to twelve? Why do you think Jesus spent more time with Peter, James, and John than He did with the other disciples? Did He like them better, or was there some other reason?** Help your kids see that Jesus seemed to know the benefits of having a small group. He could be more intimate with a circle of twelve (and even more so with a smaller group of three) than He could with huge crowds. He could train a small group to carry on after Him when He was gone. He could teach them how to relate not only to God, but to each other as well. Try to use this example to build up the members of your small group and help them become more devoted to each other.

Step 5

The Bingo activity on Repro Resource 10 won't work as well with a small group as it will with a large one. But you can accomplish the same result in a number of other ways. One option is to pair up group members who don't know each very well (if that's possible in a small group), and then have the pairs compete to see which partners can find the most (or the most unusual) common bonds. Another option is to do the same thing *as a group.* If you have four people in the group, you must find common bonds among all four. Make a list of the common bonds you discover. Then plan some fun activities based on those common bonds.

Step 3

Rather than having group members study the assigned passages, you might choose to have them act out some "friendship parables" instead. Explain that many of Jesus' parables were based on the needs and actions of friends. Have your kids form small groups. Assign each group one of Jesus' parables. Instruct the group to create a mini-play based on the parable. Among the parables you might use are the Friend in Need (Luke 11:5-10), the Good Samaritan (Luke 10:30-37), the Shrewd Manager (Luke 16:1-9), the Unmerciful Servant (Matthew 18:23-34), and the Moneylender (Luke 7:41-43). After each parable reenactment, have group members discuss what they think Jesus was saying in the parable. Also have them look for principles specifically related to friendship that they can find in these parables.

Step 4

If a major goal of friendship is to "sharpen" one another (Proverbs 27:17), a large group of friends should be filled with opportunities. To help kids find out more about such opportunities, give each person a pencil and two sheets of paper. On the first sheet of paper, he or she should make a list of "Things I frequently need help with." On the other sheet, he or she should list "Things I'm pretty good at." Both lists should be specific and detailed. When everyone finishes, collect the sheets and look for matches. For example, some kids may frequently need help with math, while others are good at figuring out and explaining math problems. Sometimes kids are reluctant to share their needs with others. But if you can foster an environment of help and support in your group, many of your members may discover that much of their confusion and suffering is in vain.

Step 1

Friendship is a fairly common topic—one that experienced youth group attenders are sure to have covered several times. To help them generate a new enthusiasm for the subject, begin the session by having kids imagine that this is the first time they're meeting. No one should know anything about anyone else. Have each person introduce himself or herself, sharing the things about his or her life that are most important. Afterward, ask: **If all you knew about anyone here is what you've just heard, who do you think you would try to make friends with first? Why?** (Some kids may be attracted to a person's sense of humor or some other characteristic. Others might pursue a common interest or hobby.) Look for surprises—people who hadn't considered themselves close friends who discover they have a lot in common. Point out that if we try to expand our circle of friends, we may discover many other people who will become just as close to us as our existing friends.

Step 2

After the Tormentors/Victim skit, ask: **Are you more frequently a Tormentor of others or a Victim? Explain. Do you think this skit needed another character? If so, whom would you have added?** Let group members respond. If no one mentions it, point out that the skit probably could have used a person or persons to stand up for the Victim. It's good that we choose not to pick on people, but it's not enough. When we see people being tormented, we need to get involved on behalf of the victim. Sometimes "heard it all before" kids have a good grasp of the black and white sides of issues, but they are likely to need help seeing the shades of gray in between and their own need to perhaps reconsider where they're drawing personal lines of responsibility.

Step 3

Most people have friends, but not everyone has thought about the *quality* of his or her friendships. Ask for three volunteers to act out the old scenario of a person trying to make a decision while a devil whispers temptations in one ear and an angel whispers good advice in the other ear. See which of the influences is more persuasive. Then, as you move into the Bible study, try to show that we need to choose our friends carefully. Point out that Jesus chose specific people to train as disciples, and those people chose to leave everything behind to follow Him. Say: **Think of all the friends you have now. Can you think of any wants or needs you have that those friendships don't fulfill?** Let kids respond. Point out the importance of having Christian friends who can help fill needs such as spiritual growth and genuine acceptance. Challenge group members to be more positive influences on the friends they currently have.

Step 4

To people with little Bible background, the concept of Jesus being a friend may be new and incredible. Have group members list all of the specific acts of friendship they've experienced during the past week: receiving gifts, having favors done, spending time together with someone, being forgiven, etc. Then, in each case, try to help them see how Jesus fulfills that same function. Even though we don't have the opportunity to relate with Him in a tangible way, His friendship is more complete and long-lasting (eternal) than any other we could ever hope for. Try to help group members discover the value of having a friend who will never give up on them—no matter what they do.

Step 3

After looking at the stories of Jesus' friendship with *one* person, Peter, have kids dwell on the *diversity* of friends Jesus had. Remind them that He was known (in an unflattering way) as "a friend of tax collectors and 'sinners'" (Matthew 11:19). Have kids name all of the people they can think of who were befriended by Jesus. The list might include His disciples (including a zealot, a tax collector, and a bunch of blue-collar workers), lepers, the woman at the well, Nicodemus (a pharisee), sick people, rich people, etc. After kids have come up with a sizable list, have them conduct a "celebration of uniqueness," in which each person thanks Jesus for his or her uniqueness. Point out that not only has God created a great diversity of people, but His Son accepts each of us equally. Then challenge kids to be more accepting of friends who are not at all like them.

Step 4

Point out that we often look forward to going out with our friends. We plan fun stuff to do, things to talk about, etc. If Jesus is truly a friend, we should do the same thing with Him. Ask group members to write out (1) specific things Jesus has done for them that they haven't thanked Him for; (2) problems they need help with or advice for; (3) concerns about other friends or family members; (4) anything else they would normally discuss with a friend. Then ask kids to think of a specific time during the next week when they can get away from phones, TVs, and stereos long enough to spend time with Jesus. Encourage them to take a Bible along as well, because Jesus often talks to us through His written Word. Attempting to relate to Jesus as a "normal" friend may feel strange to your kids at first, but assure them it will become much more natural as they practice and get used to it.

Step 1

Repro Resource 9 focuses primarily on outward or physical characteristics. So after your group members have completed the sheet, challenge them to make a list of internal qualities that they would like in a "perfect" friend. Then ask: **Do you know anyone who has all of these qualities? Do you think you'll ever know anyone who has the exact combination of qualities you described? Why or why not? What would it be like to have a friend like that?**

Step 2

During the skit, make a list of the insults that are hurled at the Victim. Then, at the end of Step 2, refer back to the list. Ask: **How do you think the Victim felt when she heard these insults? How do you think you would have felt if you were the Victim?** As a group, discuss how Jesus might have responded to each insult.

Step 2

Sometimes guys are better at losing friends than making them. So after the skit, ask each person to tell one or more "Tales of Lost Friendship." These should be true stories of why certain friendships ended. The stories should be as specific as possible. Group members should see that sometimes one person matures and outgrows a relationship. Sometimes friends move away and lose touch. Any number of valid reasons can break up a friendship. But if some of the stories include conflicts that could have been resolved, but weren't, explain that such arguments can break up relationships throughout our lives until we won't have any friends left. Challenge group members to attempt to resolve old conflicts that may still be lingering—even if they can't restore the friendship to what it was. Explain that it takes a strong person to "turn the other cheek" when offended by someone else.

Step 5

Perhaps the hardest friendships for junior high boys to make are with junior high girls. So you might skip the "Common Bond Bingo" game. (Most guys already have plenty of common interests.) Instead, have your guys brainstorm ways to strengthen their relationships with girls—as friends, not potential dating partners. (Try to keep the discussion on a very general level: **How can junior high guys get along better with junior high girls?** Otherwise, the conversation may quickly drift to who likes whom.) List suggestions on the board. Then say: **Think of three girls you know. Then think of at least one of the things we've listed that you can do to make your friendship with each girl stronger. Sometime this week try out the ideas with the girls you've chosen. Be ready to report at the next meeting and tell us what happened.** Make sure *everyone* agrees to do this. Agree as a group that anyone who fails to do this must do twice as much the following week.

Step 1

Friends experience a lot of emotions during the development of their relationships. But sometimes it's difficult to express those emotions. To demonstrate this in a fun way, assign everyone in the group a different feeling or emotion. This should be done secretly—with the emotions either written on separate sheets of paper or whispered in kids' ears. Some of the emotions might include rage, fear, love, pride, confusion, shock, disbelief, boredom, hatred, conceit, jealousy, panic, loneliness, rebellion, guilt, anxiety, and worthlessness. Have kids sit in a circle so that they can see everyone else. At your signal, simultaneously have everyone try to express his or her emotion *using facial expressions only*. Kids should try to hold their expressions so everyone else has a chance to see them. Then, one by one, let kids make their expressions while others guess what emotion the person is trying to convey.

Step 5

If the "Common Bond Bingo" game works well with your group, continue the theme on a more personal level. Have kids sit in a circle. See how far you can get around the circle building a "bonding chain." Start with any group member and the person to his or her left. The two should find something they have in common—foods, hobbies, sports teams, likes, dislikes, etc. When they decide on something, it cannot be used again by any other pair. Then the second and third persons in the circle should try to find a common bond, and so on around the circle. This will seem very easy at first, particularly following the Bingo exercise. But establish a time limit so that pairs must think quickly. Anytime a pair is unable to find a common bond within the time limit, both must drop out. Then the bonding responsibilities are passed along to the next two people. Continue until time runs out or until you reduce the group to a single winning pair.

Step 1

Friendship is a popular theme in the TV and film media. Have group members think of their favorite shows that demonstrate friendship. If possible, ask them to record key scenes ahead of time. If not, have them simply describe the friendship relationship and explain why it stands out for them. Then have them think of a TV or movie "pair" that represents their strongest friendship. (For example, a romantic friendship could be represented by *Antony and Cleopatra, Romeo and Juliet, Benny and Joon,* etc. A wacky friendship might be represented by *Beavis and Butthead.* If someone's best friend is a dog, an appropriate pair might be *Turner and Hooch.*) Encourage kids to be as creative as possible. To help them, you might want to have available some issues of *TV Guide* or movie review resources.

Step 5

As an offshoot of video dating services, have your group members create a "video friendship service." Set up a video camera in a separate room. While the meeting is going on, pull out one person at a time to sit in front of the camera and give his or her name, interests, strong points, and qualifications for friendship. At the end of the session, have everyone watch the series of clips and see the wonderful variety of friendships contained within the group.

Step 1

Rather than having everyone complete Repro Resource 9, ask two volunteers to act out a build-your-own-friend scenario. You'll need to have plenty of props and costume items available, including clothes, pillows, wigs, makeup, hair-styling gel, hairspray, eyeglasses, "instant tan" lotion, etc. Explain that one of the volunteers will play a person trying to build a "perfect" friend; the other person will play the friend he or she is trying to create. The first person will choose from Repro Resource 9 the "options" he or she wants his or her perfect friend to have. The second person will then put on the proper costume items to reflect those options. For instance, if the first person desires that his or her friend weigh 250 pounds, the second person must stuff two or three pillows under his or her shirt. If the first person desires that his or her friend have a beehive hairstyle, the second person must get to work with the styling gel and hairspray. Afterward, have your group members call out some of the things they look for in a friend.

Step 5

Obviously, the "Common Bond Bingo" game could take a long time to complete. So instead of using it, instruct each group member to find three other people in the group with whom he or she has something in common. After a minute or two, ask volunteers to share any unusual common bonds they discovered. Then as you wrap up the session, point out that looking for common bonds is one of the first steps in making new friends.

Step 2

As a group, brainstorm a list of ways in which a city kid might make an enemy of someone. Among other things, your kids might list the following actions: flashing gang signs, disputing a call in basketball, stealing someone else's boyfriend or girlfriend, spreading rumors about someone, etc. Then for each item on the list, brainstorm as a group three practical suggestions for turning that enemy into a friend. Encourage kids to write down the suggestions the group comes up with and use them as needed.

Step 5

If you don't think "Common Bond Bingo" would work well with your urban group, try a game of "Be a Friend" instead. Give each person a pad of Post-it™ notes and a pencil. After you point out that one of the reasons for Jesus' popularity was that He took the initiative in forming friendships, give your kids an opportunity to follow Jesus' example. Explain that the object of the game is to write each group member's full name (first, middle, and last)—along with something nice about that person—on a Post-it™ note, and stick the note on the person's back. The first person to complete and stick notes on all other group members is the winner. To help ensure that kids will write *sincerely* nice comments about each other, you might list trite and obvious comments on the board that kids may *not* use. These might include comments like "You're nice," "You're funny," or "You're pretty." Requiring kids to write each other's full names will ensure that they talk to each other; creating a list of "off limits" comments will help ensure that they offer genuine compliments to each other. After the game, have kids pair up. Instruct each person to read to his or her partner the comments on the partner's back.

Step 1

Combine your junior highers and high schoolers—literally. At the beginning of the session, use cords or lengths of yarn to connect high schoolers with junior highers (in pairs, or larger groups if necessary). Depending on your seating structure and planned activities, consider connecting wrists, ankles, or waists. Space should be provided for group members to maneuver without too much difficulty, but they should be close enough to be aware of each other's presence. Go through the skits, games, and other portions of the session with everyone "connected." At the end of the session, explain that just as it takes effort to operate when *literally* connected to someone else, it also takes effort to stay close to our friends, and to reach beyond our usual circle of acquaintances to include other people—especially those who may be older or younger than we are.

Step 5

Since you have junior highers and high schoolers in the same group, let the members of each age-group serve as "experts" to represent the opinions of all people their age. Ask your experts to compile a list of specific things members of the *other* age-group need to do if they want to be friends with the experts' age-group. For example, ask your junior highers what high schoolers need to do to get along better with junior highers. You might want to have them fill in the blanks of a sentence like "If high schoolers really want to be friends with junior highers, they would stop _____ and start _____." After junior highers put together their list of what high schoolers should and shouldn't do, have the high schoolers list the things junior highers need to do to be better friends with the older age-group. Both groups may come up with some surprises about things they like and don't like.

Step 1

Instead of using Repro Resource 9 to let individuals design perfect friends, work as a group (or groups) to do the same thing in person. Let one person from each group be the "prototype" for the perfect friend you're building. He or she should stand next to a wall as other group members write out criteria on pieces of paper, and either tape them to the wall behind the person or attach them in appropriate places on the person's clothing or body. ("A loving heart" would be attached to a shirt pocket; "Encouragement" would go near the mouth; etc.) Since you're dealing with real people, you should focus more on desired qualities and characteristics rather than physical attributes. Look for instances in which group members disagree on desired traits. Such differences of opinion are likely to be areas you need to deal with during the session that follows.

Step 4

As you talk about having "sharpening" friends, and of how Jesus is a friend, you might want to provide a lasting reminder of how important these things are. Many sixth graders enjoy craft activities, and friendship bracelets are currently popular. You might want to provide the materials and let group members make bracelets, rings, or some other token of friendship that they could take home as a tangible reminder of the things they discuss during the meeting. If the items you make are "cool" enough, the kids are likely to wear them to school as well, which not only helps them remember why they made them, but also creates attention and curiosity about your youth group.

Date Used:

Approx. Time

Step 1: Friendship Criteria _____
o Extra Action
o Heard It All Before
o Mostly Girls
o Extra Fun
o Media
o Short Meeting Time
o Combined Jr. High/High School
o Sixth Grade

Step 2: Dream Come True? _____
o Heard It All Before
o Mostly Girls
o Mostly Guys
o Urban

Step 3: A Friend in Deed _____
o Extra Action
o Small Group
o Large Group
o Little Bible Background
o Fellowship & Worship

Step 4: Friends in High Places _____
o Large Group
o Little Bible Background
o Fellowship & Worship
o Sixth Grade

Step 5: Common Bond Bingo _____
o Small Group
o Mostly Guys
o Extra Fun
o Media
o Short Meeting Time
o Urban
o Combined Jr. High/High School

Custom Curriculum Critique

Please take a moment to fill out this evaluation form, rip it out, fold it, tape it, and send it back to us. This will help us continue to customize products for you. Thanks!

1. Overall, please give this *Custom Curriculum* course (*What Would Jesus Do?*) a grade in terms of how well it worked for you. (A=excellent; B=above average; C=average; D=below average; F=failure) Circle one.

   A   B   C   D   F

2. Now assign a grade to each part of this curriculum that you used.

a. Upfront article	A	B	C	D	F	Didn't use
b. Publicity/Clip art	A	B	C	D	F	Didn't use
c. Repro Resource Sheets	A	B	C	D	F	Didn't use
d. Session 1	A	B	C	D	F	Didn't use
e. Session 2	A	B	C	D	F	Didn't use
f. Session 3	A	B	C	D	F	Didn't use
g. Session 4	A	B	C	D	F	Didn't use
h. Session 5	A	B	C	D	F	Didn't use

3. How helpful were the options?
   - ❏ Very helpful
   - ❏ Somewhat helpful
   - ❏ Not too helpful
   - ❏ Not at all helpful

4. Rate the amount of options:
   - ❏ Too many
   - ❏ About the right amount
   - ❏ Too few

5. Tell us how often you used each type of option (4=Always; 3=Sometimes; 2=Seldom; 1=Never)

	4	3	2	1
Extra Action	❏	❏	❏	❏
Combined Jr. High/High School	❏	❏	❏	❏
Urban	❏	❏	❏	❏
Small Group	❏	❏	❏	❏
Large Group	❏	❏	❏	❏
Extra Fun	❏	❏	❏	❏
Heard It All Before	❏	❏	❏	❏
Little Bible Background	❏	❏	❏	❏
Short Meeting Time	❏	❏	❏	❏
Fellowship and Worship	❏	❏	❏	❏
Mostly Guys	❏	❏	❏	❏
Mostly Girls	❏	❏	❏	❏
Media	❏	❏	❏	❏
Extra Challenge (High School only)	❏	❏	❏	❏
Sixth Grade (Jr. High only)	❏	❏	❏	❏

6. What did you like best about this course?

7. What suggestions do you have for improving *Custom Curriculum*?

8. Other topics you'd like to see covered in this series:

9. Are you?
    ❑ Full time paid youthworker
    ❑ Part time paid youthworker
    ❑ Volunteer youthworker

10. When did you use *Custom Curriculum*?
    ❑ Sunday School   ❑ Small Group
    ❑ Youth Group   ❑ Retreat
    ❑ Other _____

11. What grades did you use it with? _____

12. How many kids used the curriculum in an average week? _____

13. What's the approximate attendance of your entire Sunday school program (Nursery through Adult)? _____

14. If you would like information on other *Custom Curriculum* courses, or other youth products from David C. Cook, please fill out the following:

Name: _____

Church Name: _____

Address: _____

_____

Phone: (_____) _____

Thank you!